Apṛthak-Siddhibhāva

With Special Reference to Rāmānuja's Metaphysics

Other Book by the Same Author

1. Karma: Freedom and Responsibility, 1998

Apṛthak-Siddhibhāva

With Special Reference to Rāmānuja's Metaphysics

Aparna Chakraborty

2001

Kaveri Books

New Delhi - 110 002

ISBN 81-7479-049-7
First Published in 2001
Price: Rs. 260

Published by
Rakesh Goel
Kaveri Books,
4697/5-21 A, Ansari Road,
New Delhi - 110 002 (India).
Tel. 328 8140, 324 5799 Fax: 011 719 9029
e.mail: kaveribook@vsnl.com

Printed at:
Chawla Offset Printers, Delhi - 110 052.

PRINTED IN INDIA

Dedicated

to

My Father

Sri Chandrakumar Chakraborty

Contents

Preface

The philosophy of Vedānta is rooted in the *Upaniṣads,* the *Bhagavad-gītā* and the *Brahma-sūtras* of Bādarāyaṇa. These three are technically known as *prasthānatraya*, which constitutes the foundation as well as the supreme authority of the Vedānta philosophy. Every great *ācārya*, who spoke in the name of the Vedāntic philosophy, therefore, found it necessary to write commentary on the *prasthānatraya*.

Crystallized in the chief commentaries on the *prasthānatraya,* Śaṁkarás Advaita and Rāmānuja's Viśiṣṭādvaita are the most striking and thought provoking expositions. Both Śaṁkara and Rāmānuja started with different philosophical standpoints to represent different types of Vedāntic philosophy. Śaṁkara's philosophy focussed on the non-relational reality. The non-relational reality of Śaṁkara is nothing but a pure identity *(tādātmya)*. It is a pure identity because the world of conscious selves *(jīva)* is non-different from Brahman, while the world of the non-conscient objects *(jagat)* is a mere 'illusion' *(māyā)*. Advaita thus denies relation on the ground that, if there should be relation *(bhāva)* then there will also have to be difference *(bheda)*. For relational consciousness presupposes a differential consciousness, too. Hence Brahman for Śaṁkara is differenceless, therefore, relationless *(abheda)*. Advaitin argues that all differences, therefore, all relations, are ultimately unreal.

Rāmānuja, on the other hand, thinks that the denial of relations would infact reduce all things to nullity. Reality, to Rāmānuja, too, in a sense, is the non-dual spirit *(advaya)*. But it is not a distinctionless homogeneous identity *(nirviśeṣa-tādātmya)*, as it is to Advaita. For Rāmānuja, the ultimate reality cannot be a bare undifferentiated unity, but a unity that contains and admits, as such, differences which are all real. All differences, and all distinctions, for that matter, are deep within the heart of it. They are also not left unorganised, but are harmoniously co-ordinated. The differences are co-eval and co-eternal with the unity of the reality. Thus Rāmānuja rejects the absolutistic principle of bare identity and affirms a living principle of differentiation at the very heart of reality. Rāmānuja's absolute then is a concrete individual. It is an identity achieved in and through difference. Thus the relation of difference is fundamental to Rāmānuja's philosophy. For Rāmānuja pure identity, or pure being without any differentiation, is a metaphysical fiction. Rāmānuja's Brahman is not a non-differentiated pure being. On the contrary, his Brahman possesses an internal difference *(svagata-bheda)* within itself, since it is internally related with the objective world *(acit-prapañca)* as well as the subjective world *(cit-prapañca)*. The relation, that holds good between Brahman and the objective world, on the one hand, and between Brahman and the subjective world, on the other, is an inner, inseparable, vital and organic relation. Such a relation is called by Rāmānuja as *apṛthak-siddhibhāva*. The relation of *apṛthak-siddhi*, in a sense, is the central point around which Rāmānuja's whole philosophy revolves. It should be both possible and fruitful to view Rāmānuja's metaphysics through the perspective of this unique relation of inseparability. This book is a critical analysis of this *apṛthak-siddhi-bhāva* and its application in Rāmānuja's metaphysics.

It gives me great pleasure to acknowledge my deep indebtedness to my revered teacher Dr. C.R. Agera, under whose supervision and guidance I completed this work. I am deeply indebted to my other teacher Dr. Jagat Pal for his guidance and help in all my efforts.

I am greatly thankful to my teachers Dr. S.C. Daniel, Prof. Sujata Miri and Prof. Mrinal Miri who have encouraged me in this work. I am deeply thankful to my teacher Dr. Raghunath Ghosh (Dept. of Philosophy, University of North Bengal) for his valuable suggestion whenever needed.

I express my thanks and gratitude to Mr. Joseph F. Khongbuh (Dept. of C.I.E.F.L. North-Eastern Hill University) for his constant help and encouragement. My sincere thanks go to my other well wishers for their help and support in accomplishing this task. Lastly I would like to express my heartiest thanks to the publisher Kaveri Books, New Delhi for publishing this book.

Aparna Chakraborty

whose supervision and guidance I completed this work. I am deeply indebted to my other teacher Dr. Jagat Pal for his guidance and help in all my efforts.

I am greatly thankful to my teachers Dr. S. C. Daniel, Prof. Sujata Miri and Prof. [illegible] Miri who have encouraged me in this work. I am deeply thankful to my teacher Dr. [illegible] (Dept. of Philosophy, University of North [illegible]) for his valuable suggestion whenever needed.

I express my thanks and gratitude to Mr. Joseph J. Khonglah (Dept. of C.I.T.E.T., North Eastern Hill University) for his constant help and encouragement. My sincere thanks go to my other well wishers for their help and support in accomplishing this task. Lastly I would like to express my heartfelt thanks to the publisher Kaveri Books New Delhi for publishing this book.

Aparna Chakraborty

1

Introduction

Viśiṣṭādvaita Vedānta of Rāmānuja, for all its differences with Śaṁkara's views on reality, is in a sense, a form of non-dualistic (*advaita*) philosophy; but it is a non-dualism of the qualified (*viśiṣṭasya advaita*). Indeed, in every school of Vedānta, an ultimacy and supremacy is ascribed to Brahman, the metaphysical highest, consistent with the spirit of the triple sources (*prasthāna-traya*) of the Vedāntic philosophy. They are the *Upaniṣads*, the *Bhagavad-gītā* and the *Brahma-sūtras* of Bādarāyaṇa, the basic *sūtras* of the founder of the Vedāntic school. These three sources supposedly represent the school's commitment to *śruti, smṛti* and *tarka*. Thus, Vedānta represents within itself a methodology based on scripture, tradition and reason. It is therefore at once an exegesis, culture and philosophy. Through all of them Vedānta reflects on the nature of reality. Every great *ācārya*, who spoke in the name of the Vedāntic philosophy, therefore found it necessary to comment on the *prasthānatraya*. In the process they came up with their own specific understanding of the nature of the ultimate reality. A problem that they all had to face is the following:

If Brahman is the ultimate reality, how are the other realities, both of the order of the conscient *(cit)* and of the non-conscient *(acit)*, related to the metaphysical highest? It is precisely on this question that the Vedāntic schools widely differ. The classical formulation of Śaṁkara here has been the affirmation of not only the ultimacy but also the *sole* reality of Brahman. This affirmation has been so uncompromising that the world of conscious selves is said to be non-different from Brahman, while the world of the non-conscient objects is further said to be a mere 'illusion' *(māyā)*.

This classical Advaitic formulation is contested by Rāmānuja. He would rather see here that the ultimacy of Brahman only affirms the supremacy of Brahman without cancelling the reality of the individual selves and the objects. The latter are included in the former not merely as spatio-temporal phases but as its eternal and co-eval modes *(prakāra)*. They are indeed related inseparably *(apṛthak-siddhi-bhāva)* with Brahman as the modes of the latter. Hence, the relation of inseparability is fundamental to Rāmānuja's metaphysics. Even a cursory glance through the *Śrībhāṣya*, the *magnum opus,* of Rāmānuja, gives me the impression that *apṛthak-siddhi* is a convenient relational category that Rāmānuja employs in the explication of his rich metaphysics. It is perhaps both possible and fruitful to view Rāmānuja's metaphysics through the perspective of this unique relation of inseparability. Such a study, I am inclined to believe, will not only throw new light on Rāmānuja's metaphysics, but also may be some kind of a help to set a few correctives to some of the most misunderstood categories of Indian philosophy, in general, but also of Rāmānuja's Viśiṣṭādvaita, in particular. Thus, for example, the union of 'soul-body' as applied to the (human) psycho-physical organism, or to god as the highest and the all inclusive reality, generally viewed with suspicion, can be now seen more positively. This is only one such insight of this new approach to Viśiṣṭādvaita. This book is a critical analysis of this *apṛthak-siddhi-bhāva* and its application in Rāmānuja's metaphysics.

Surveying through Rāmānuja Vedānta, I see works in the area of epistemology, metaphysics, philosophy of religion (under the nomenclature of ethics); but there hardly is any study worth the name on the nature of any type of relation in this philosopher, who may be said to be truly a philosopher of relatedness. We must not further ignore the important fact that, due to the sway that Advaita has held in our academics, it has become almost synonymous with a living philosophy of Vedānta to the western consciousness, at least; a philosophy of relatedness within the Vedāntic tradition smacks of a certain suspicion. And yet, a philosophy of relatedness is what makes for any sort of social and political philosophy. Little wonder, then, that the charge that Vedānta is an other-worldly philosophy, sundered from the socio-political concerns, has gained credence; in vain have the scholars, trying to prove that the realized person *(mukta)* is only a-social but not anti-social, succeeded in dispelling one's suspicions here. I begin to reflect on a dominant trend of philosophy of relatedness, within the Vedāntic tradition itself. An analysis of the particular type of relation, that holds good between Brahman, the self and the non-self, and its application in Rāmānuja's metaphysics then should be of fundamental importance to any form of Vedāntic social philosophy. To be sure, I will not enter into the concerns of social philosophy here, but I hope to prepare a ground for it through my metaphysical study in this book.

In a study of the analysis of the nature of *apṛthak-siddhattva* and its application in metaphysics, it is desirable that one begins with the category of relation itself in Indian philosophy. A brief discussion on the concept of relation *(bhāva)* in Indian philosophy in general therefore would facilitate me to approach the problem with a proper perspective. Naiyāyikas understanding of relation here is of paramount importance. They are after all the pioneers of Indian epistemology. It is they who have carried on incisive analysis on the concept of relation. For my purpose, I shall dwell at some length on their concept of conjunction *(saṁyoga)* and inherence *(samavāya)*. This is because, while we can make a clear distinction between conjunction and inherence, the latter category of inherence has much in common with the *apṛthak-siddhi* relation of Rāmānuja. Scholars have tended to identify *samavāya* of the Naiyāyikas with the *apṛthak-siddhi* of Rāmānuja. In my examination, I hope to show that similarities between the two types of relations not withstanding, they cannot be identified. Any such identification would do violence to Rāmānuja's organismic understanding of reality. It would also be worth pursuing, here, if organismic model that Rāmānuja adopts in his metaphysics is realistic or merely religious, admitting many layers of symbolic meanings.

Yet another question that will be concerned here is a comparison, brief though it is, of *apṛthak-siddhattva* with the Buddhist and the Advaitic conception of *tādātmya*. Such a comparison is found to be necessary, in the context of the pervasiveness in Indian philosophy of *satkāryavāda* and *vivartavāda,* that have, in varying degrees, tended to view substantive-attributive relations, in the ultimate analysis, to be a relation of identity. While Advaita Vedānta may be motivated to do this for safeguarding the absolute oneness of Brahman, the Buddhist is constrained here both by his epistemological and metaphysical considerations. It is of interest to note how Rāmānuja's *apṛthak-siddhattva,* while subscribing to a form of *brahma-pariṇāmavāda*, therefore a form of *satkāryavāda,* still steers clear off Advaita and Buddhism. The above analysis of Advaitic position will however have to be subjected to an in-depth study. This is all the more important to me, since Rāmānuja enters into a rather detailed refutation of Advaitin's rejection of the concept of relation itself *(bheda-dhikkāra)*. And, this is not without reason. For, once the concept of relation is shown to be riddled with internal contradictions, the book can be extended to any type of relation, *apṛthak-siddhi* included. This indeed is what Advaitin aims at, although he is not much concerned with *apṛthak-siddhattva* itself. But if Rāmānuja's metaphysics should mean anything at all, he has first of all to establish the validity of relation itself. In my opinion, Rāmānuja has proved equal to the philosophical task.

He therefore turns his attention to the Vedāntic notion of *bheda* as a *bhāva*, more particularly, as conceived in Advaita Vedānta. Needless to say, either its rejection or acceptance is determined by the types of vision of metaphysical reality. Why did Rāmānuja feel the need of rejecting *sajātīya-bheda* and *vijātīya-bheda*, but affirm the paramount importance of *svagata-bheda*? This is a question that needs a careful philosophical analysis. For herein is Rāmānuja's sympathy with a Vedāntic non-dualism and, yet, his rejection of a pure non-dualism. It is true, in order to maintain the absolute unity of Brahman, he rules out, along with Advaitin, *sajātīya-bheda*, for there is no being that is similar (similarity of species) to Brahman. Brahman is not one of a class. Likewise, in order to maintain Brahman's uniqueness, he rules out, again along with Advaitin, *vijātīya-bheda*, for there is no being that is entirely dissimilar to Brahman. Brahman is not a being unto oneself as distinct from other beings unto themselves. But, in order to maintain an organismic unity between Brahman, *cit* and *acit*, he affirms, may it be noted, as against Advaitin, *svagata-bheda,* for *cit* and *acit* are within Brahman distinct and yet inseparable from Brahman. I have addressed myself here to a number of questions: Can one logically maintain Advaitin's rejection of the relation itself *(bheda/bhāva-dhikkāra)*? Rāmānuja, if he felt the need for *svagata-bheda*, has his own reasons, not only in virtue of a coherence in his metaphysics; he also proves himself to be not less of a metaphysician in meeting the challenges of the Advaitins here.

Once the theoretical issues concerning the nature of relation and also a critique of Advaitini's critique of relation are treated, I take up the application of the relation of inseparability in Rāmānuja's metaphysics. First, I take up the application of *apṛthak-siddhattva* to the relation between

Brahman and *acit prapañca*. *Acit*, to Rāmānuja is a mode of Brahman, related by the relation of inseparability. In rest of Vedānta, this inconscient aspect of reality is treated as the principle of *māyā* that makes possible the evolution of the world from Brahman. Rāmānuja rarely uses this much-maligned word for the principle of potentiality. When he does use, it is without any derogatory connotation. The principle of potentiality is neither *māyā* nor *avidyā,* a principle that fabricates a world of illusion with a status of a secondary and a derivative reality. Here, he is much closer to Sāṁkhya than any other Vedāntin is. Rather *acit* is *prakṛti* that is not in a relation of antagonism with Puruṣottama within an organismic philosophy; there hardly is a room for an internal or external opposition between spirit and matter. In Rāmānuja, we do not encounter either the dualism of matter and spirit, or their parallelism; matter as the principle of becoming has its locus within the heart of the spirit. The spirit evolves in the sense of making manifest whatever is unmanifest within it; the manifest world is a self-unfolding of the eternal spirit while the principle of becoming itself is a mode of Brahman.

I have addressed myself to a number of questions that can be raised at this juncture. Can *acit*, in so far as it is *jaḍa* adequately reflect Brahman that is a conscient reality? If not, what is gained in admitting the substantive- attributive relation between these two? What is the type of causality that Rāmānuja subscribes to? Has Rāmānuja sacrificed the purity of Brahman by making Brahman both *upādāna* and *nimitta-kāraṇa*? I am afraid Rāmānuja's answers here may be, to some extent, unsatisfactory to a philosopher. But we cannot forget that Rāmānuja is a Vedāntic hermeneutician. I hope I have something to say on this in the concluding part of the book. Yet another problem that arises here, but which I have only casually touched upon in this book is this: *acit-prapañca* is constituted of the five elements *(pañcīkaraṇa),* as it is generally understood elsewhere in Indian philosophy. And yet, Rāmānuja's doctrine of the world may be said to be a doctrine of triplication *(trivṛtkaraṇa)*. Has *apṛthak-siddhattva* anything to do with this discordant note struck by Rāmānuja in Indian cosmology? I am inclined to see Rāmānuja's dependence on *śruti* much more here than elsewhere. It is not merely a fascination of the triple realities of *puruṣa, cit* and *acit*, or merely a desire to trace the world process to the constituents of *sattva, rajas* and *tamas* of *prakṛti:* it is rather to remain closest to the oldest tradition within the *Veda*.

A second case of application of *apṛthak-siddhattva,* and a more important one at that, is between Brahman and *cit-prapañca*, the world of the conscient selves, in Rāmānuja's metaphysics. This is more important because it was the consideration of acknowledging self's autonomy within the divine scheme that made Rāmānuja formulate his qualified non-dualism. In this way, man is at the heart of his philosophy of *tattva-traya*. Again, it is this consideration of safeguarding the autonomy of the individual selves from its total merger into the essence of the metaphysical highest of the *nirguṇa-brahman* in liberation, that made Rāmānuja to carry on a scathing attack on pure Advaita. However, there are a number of issues here that call for a detailed and careful analysis: First of all there are those beautiful models of the relation that obtain between Brahman and *cit*, such as *ādhāra-ādheya, śeṣī-śeṣa, niyantṛ-niyāmya dhārtṛ-dhārya, aṁśi-aṁśa, guṇī-guṇa* and so on. Every one of these models brings out either a deep metaphysical or epistemological or aesthetical, at times, even a ritualistic, aspect of Rāmānuja's philosophy. I also show the impact of *Karma-Mīmāṁsā* too on Vedāntic *ācārya* Rāmānuja, that has gone totally ignored in Advaita. The models employed have brought Rāmānuja's metaphysics closer to the heart of the philosophers of religion, and the Vaiṣṇava theologians too, and served as a powerful impetus to the medieval *bhakti-paramparā* of India. This is partly because Rāmānuja does not indulge in the distinction between Brahman and Īśvara, *nirguṇa* and *saguṇa;* to him the metaphysical and the religious highest are one and the same. This he does without sacrificing in the least the transcendental character of Brahman. And yet, what is closer to his philosophy of religion is not *paratva*, or *īśītṛtva*, of Brahman but *saulabhya* and *antaryāmītva*. All this is made possible because of the resilient application of *apṛthak-siddhattva* in Rāmānuja's metaphysics.

Other philosophical problems that deserve our attention are: human freedom vis-a-vis the will of the supreme Brahman; the status of the individual self both in bondage and liberation alike. His views on human freedom may not be philosophically satisfactory. Nonetheless, within a religious matrix it does make an eminent sense. For to a *bhakta* or *kiṁkara,* in virtue of the *apṛthak-siddhattva*, there cannot be ontologically a freedom from Brahman but only a freedom in Brahman. Understood in this sense, Rāmānuja fully upholds the moral freedom of *cit*.

It would be of some interest to pursue the type of relation, that obtains between Śrī and Brahman, specially the applicability or otherwise of *apṛthak-siddhattva*. Does the relation finally break down here? I only raise the question here with the hope that some philosopher of the religion would pay some attention to it; it however falls outside the purview of my study.

Finally, in the concluding part of the study I have highlighted Rāmānuja's hermeneutical concerns in the employment of *apṛthak-siddhi-bhāva*. I am afraid, this attempt is rather sketchy. However, instead of merely summing up my results, I have tried to bring out the implications of the type of methodology that Rāmānuja follows as a Vedāntin. After all, Vedānta is a kind of hermeneutics, a form of scriptural exegesis. But this scriptural exegesis is not antithetical to the employment of the categories of reason or tradition. He makes use of them to the fullest extent, and yet he operates within the basic presupposition of the *upaniṣadic* philosophy leaving here ample scope for manifold interpretation.

The method that I have followed is descriptive, analytical and comparative. Descriptive because I want to see meaning into what Rāmānuja so insightfully writes; analytical because I wanr to see the philosophical significance of Rāmạnuja's metaphysics, from a limited perspective though; comparative because I believe that Rāmānuja's metaphysics will be better understood when it is projected against other schools of Indian metaphysics, Advaita Vedānta in particular. The study is based primarily on the three works of Rāmānuja, the *Śrībhāṣya,* the *Vedārtha-saṁgraha* and the *Gītābhāṣya*, with a greater reliance on the *Śrībhāṣya* and the secondary sources wherever they would corroborate the understanding of Rāmānuja's metaphysics.

2

Apṛthak-Siddhi and Philosophy of Relation

Relation is an important element in any system of philosophy, Eastern or Western. For without the concept of relation neither epistemology nor metaphysics of that system can meaningfully speak of its basic problems. This is because philosophy enquires into the nature of the universe, the nature of the human soul and its destiny, and the nature of God or the Absolute, not in isolation but in their *relation* to one another. Again, it also enquires into the nature of matter, time, space, causality, evolution, life and mind, again, not merely in isolation but in their relation to one another. Likewise, any epistemological query has to probe into the realities of the knowing subject, the object known, the instruments through which the process of knowledge takes place and the phenomenon of knowledge itself. However, whatever the analytic approach, when knowledge is seen finally as a synthetic product, the various elements of knowledge will have to be seen in their relation to one another. Therefore the concept of relation becomes important for philosophy. In this chapter, I would like to set Rāmānuja's concept of *apṛthaksiddhi-bhāva* within the general context of a philosophy of relation in Indian philosophy.

Among all the schools of Vedānta, Śaṁkara's Advaita and Rāmānuja's Viśiṣṭādvaita are conspicuous on the issue of relation, the former for its militant rejection of relation, and the latter for its ardent advocacy of the same. Surprisingly both the attitudes are occasioned by their concern to explicate the nature of the ultimate reality. Advaita upholds the view that reality is non-relational; the non-relational reality is nothing but a pure identity *(brahma-satyam)*. It is pure-identity because the world of conscious selves is non-different from Brahman *(jīvo-brahmaiva-nā paraḥ)*, while the world of the non-conscient objects is a mere 'illusion' *(jagan-mithyā)*. This is the quintessence of Advaitic metaphysics.

Rāmānuja, on the other hand, is of the view that Reality, if it were not to be abstract, cannot but be relational. Hence, he takes upon himself both to oppose and criticise Advaitic pure identity. He argues out that Reality cannot be a pure identity; on the contrary, it must be a 'concrete individual' or 'concrete identity'. And the 'concrete identity' of Brahman is possible only in and through the different conscious selves *(cit)* and non-conscient objects *(acit)*. *Cit* and *acit* are *related* inseparably *(apṛthaksiddhi-bhāva)* with Brahman, as the latter's mode. If Brahman is the substance, the world of selves and the objects constitute its attributes or modes. If so, the relation that exists between the substantive Brahman and the attributive self and the non-self is one of inseparability. Therefore the relation of inseparability *(apṛthak-siddhi-bhāva)* may be said to constitute the pivot on which Rāmānuja's whole philosophy turns. To Rāmānuja, *apṛthaksiddhi* is an inner, inseparable, vital and organic relation. Such a relation holds between substance and its attribute, between body and soul, between part and whole and also between one substance and another substance. By implication it now follows that the relation concerned 'connotes that one of the two entities related is dependent upon the other in the sense that one cannot exist without the other also existing, and that it cannot be rightly known without the other also being known at the same time.'[1] It also indicates that the relation that we are speaking of here has both metaphysical and epistemological bearings. What is more, it also indicates that explication of the concept of relation is a *sine qua non* for a realist, before he can proceed for its application in his philosophy. I hope to elaborate on these implications. In the entire gamut of Indian philosophy, it is the Naiyāyikas, the radical realists that they are, who have carried on a searching analysis, on the concept of relation.

The word relation literally means a 'bringing together' What do we bring together? There should at least be two terms, if we are to speak meaningfully of relation. The terms need not be, strictly speaking, the objective entities, although this often is the case to the realists, it is sufficient even if they are *mens rea*, irrespective of the fact whether these mental realities have a foundation in reality or not. The Sanskrit word *bhāva* clearly includes within itself not only any existent thing, object or substance but also an idea, disposition, thought or supposition.[2] It now may be thought that relation is what brings together the two terms, irrespective of their ontological status. To the Naiyāyikas however, because of their radical realism, all relation is between their categories *(padārthas)* of substance *(dravya)*, quality *(guṇa)*, action *(karma)*, generality *(sāmānya)*, particularity *(viśeṣa)*, inherent *(samavāya)* and non-existence *(abhāva)*. This is partly because, to the Naiyāyikas, all relations are real things, or real 'meanings', having their objective reality and validity. Of these categories, what is of particular interest to me here is *samavāya*, which is an important relation of inherence that exists between a substance *(dravya)* and such other categories as quality, action etc. as it has certain similarities with Rāmānuja's *apṛthaksiddhi-bhāva*.

Samavāya, to Nyāya, is an inseparable and eternal relation between two non-pervasive entities, of which one is said to inhere in the other. Such a relation holds good in a number of instances: The whole is in its parts; a quality or an action is in a substance; the universal is in the individual; and the particularity is in some simple eternal substance or atoms. Thus we say that the cloth, as a whole, is in its threads; the colour 'red', as a quality, is in the rose; motion, as an action, belongs to the moving ball; manhood, as a universal, is in individual man; and finally, the particularity, or the distinctive character, of one mind or soul is in that mind or soul.

All these are instantiations that Nyāya place before us for the relation of inherence. The inherent cannot exist independent of the inhered substance. Nor can you know the inherent independent of the inhered substance. Nyāya is quite consistent here in presuming that our categories of knowledge are delimited by the objects of knowledge *(mānādhīnameya)*.

Naiyāyika is quick to point out that the relation of inherence *(samavāya)* is different from conjunction *(saṁyoga)*, because the latter is a temporary, or non-eternal, relation between two things; the two things or the relation in conjunction, usually exist in separation from each other. Once the relation is established between them, they are temporarily brought together. For example, two balls moving from opposite directions meet at a certain place; the relation which holds between them, when they meet, is one of conjunction; it is temporary. They can once again be separated at one's sweet pleasure. Therefore, the conjunction to the Naiyāyikas is, strictly speaking, a relation that is at once a quality of the terms related by it; it is not a relation of inherence.

On the other hand, *samavāya* is an inseparable and eternal relation between the relata. Here, the whole is *always* related to its parts, if we speak of the relation between the whole and its parts; a quality or an action is *always* related to some substance, if we speak of the relation between a substance and its attributes. So long as the whole exists, it must exist in the parts; so also, a quality or action exists so long as the substance in which it inheres exists. Such is also the case with the relation that obtains between the universal and its individual, between the particularity and its simple eternal substance. Thus we see that the relation, of a whole to its parts, of any quality or action to its substance, of the universal to the individual, and of particularity to the eternal substances, is one of inherence; and that it is not produced by the conjunction of two separate things.

We should be careful to note the one-sidedness of dependence in the relation of inherence. For it may be an eternal relation between any two entities, one of which cannot exist without the other, but the terms related by *samavāya* cannot be reversed at our sweet pleasure. It is the inherent that is dependent on the inhered; the independence of the inhered substance is implicit in the Naiyāyikas definition of *dravya* itself. In contradistinction with this relation of inherence, the terms related by conjunction *(saṁyoga)* can be reversed at our pleasure. For in this readjustment there is a constant disjunction and conjunction in virtue of the temporal character. For example, if there is a contact of the hand with a pen, the pen also must be in contact with the hand. This relation of conjunction is not so much a case of one thing being in the other as one thing being in contact with the other. But the latter is the case when we say that the cloth is in the threads, or sweetness is in the mango. Here the relation is manifestly one-sided dependence, for though a quality is in a substance, the substance is not in the quality.

Nyāya further holds that, though there can be more than one instantiation of *samavāya, samavāya* is not many. It is a single relation of inherence. This is because the same distinguishing feature characterises the different instantiations. One *samavāya* is sufficient to relate all its relata, while conjunctions are many, since they are all characterized by temporal contacts, here the ordering of contacts can be varied.

In each case the ordering of the parts is different. But in the relation of inherence, there is no variety of the ordering of the parts; inherence is more than an external contact. Further, *samavāya* is not produced by any cause; it is uncaused: hence it is an eternal relation. *Samavāya* is imperceptible, whereas *saṁyoga* is said to be perceptible. For we see things temporarily coming together and going asunder due to the external causality, but we do not perceive the relation of inherence; rather through it we understand the mode of being. On the other hand, conjunction is caused. Conjunction is also destroyed by disjunction of its relata: it is purely temporary. Being temporary, conjunction is an adventitious relation, whereas *samavāya* is a natural relation. All these differences have made the Naiyāyikas to assign conjunction only the status of a quality, whereas *samavāya* is given the status of a separate category *(padārtha)*.

But, the attempt of Nyāya in explicating the nature of relation, in particular, that of the relation of inherence, has not gone unchallenged. It has been severely criticised by the Mādhyamika and the Yogācāra Buddhists. I am inclined to believe that both the views of Nyāya and their Buddhist opponents are dictated by the type of metaphysics that they subscribe to. For, whereas the Naiyāyikas have allowed a true play of radical realism here, the Buddhists have attacked realism and are dictated by metaphysical idealism, have ended up with a kind of nominalism, which denied the objective reality to the category of inherence. Let me briefly state this position, if for nothing, but to highlight the realistic inclination of Rāmānuja in subscribing to *apṛthaksiddhi-bhāva*, as against all metaphysical idealisms.

Both Yogācāra and Mādhyamika Buddhists are of the view that all relations are external realities. *Eo ipso,* the category of inherence, which is also a unique relation, does not have any link with the substances in which they are supposed to inhere. They are therefore nothing but a subjective fiction. The notions of the genus and the species, of substance and attribute etc., are all fictitious without corresponding realities. Indeed, there are no substances at all that fit into the definitions given by Nyāya, an eternal, changeless reality. Substances, no less than the relation of inherence, are all names devised by mind that are merely vacuous. For these names are inapplicable to reality that, at any rate, cannot be grasped by the categorial modes of knowing. But, in arriving at this same conclusion, Mādhyamikas and Yogācāras take different paths with different presuppositions.

The Mādhyamika Buddhist reject every type of relation, because to them reality is non-relational. That means reality is nothing but 'thing-in-itself',[3] a 'point instant'. It is a genuine, unique, independent and intimate reality, that transcends all categorial modes of knowing. Their ultimate reality, *śūnyatā,* is not rational; if not rational, all the attributes that we give to it, all the relations that we conceive of in regard to the transcendental reality do not hold good, it is in an unrelated reality. They deny relations, in particular, because they believe that all relations are constructed *(kalpanā)*. Relations and constructions are one and the same, and they are the fabrications of our imagination, whereas the ultimate reality exists in itself, and not in virtue of being constructed. It is the mathematical point instant. Once all relations are in this way discarded, one is impelled to conceive it as a pure identity, or *tādātmya.* According to Dignāga, all relations are inferred and, as such, they are constructed by our understanding. For such inferred relations are based on our understanding of substance-quality combination, whereas a relational substance does not represent ultimate reality at all.

The above work of the Mādhyamika is explicable to us only against the backdrop of their absolutism. The categorizations of the contingent world cannot apply to the Absolute. Relations have a contingent reality, therefore they cannot hold good in respect of the ultimate reality. Ultimate reality is non-relative absolute, which is independent; its counterpart is merely empirical, it is imagined reality; only the latter is interrelated and interdependent, but the former is relationless. Even from the epistemic enterprises, Digñāga draws our attention to the Mādhyamika thesis that, in the very final stage, that is, the Absolute stage, the distinction between the subject and the object is so overcome that they become united. Therefore in the end stage, there remains no difference at all. The difference is only an appearance, an undifferentiated object appears differentiated only through illusion. Whatever difference that is initially experienced is true only for the empirical world. But this view *(dṛṣṭi)* cannot give us an Absolute reality that is non-differentiated. This attempt to the Mādhyamikas is basically metaphysical in flavour. They proceed with the assumption that the ultimate reality is *śūnyatā*. It is *śūnyatā* because it is the negation of all our attributions which are the vacuous constructions of our understanding. The truth consists in the denudation of the mental constructs that do not apply to the Absolute.

The Yogācāras, on the other hand, are unmistakably idealists in their approach. They refute to locate the ultimate reality outside the mental; consciousness itself is the ultimate and absolute reality. All divisions within the all-absorbing consciousness are to be overcome. In the process of overcoming divisions, their axe, first of all, falls on the mental relations. They had nothing to fight, after all, outside the mental realm. Accordingly, Dharmakīrti says that the essence of consciousness is undivided, because consciousness is self-transparent and self-luminous and does not connote any subject-object relation in its construction. The distinction between the subject and the object is an illusive division within. Ultimate reality, being a single unit of the nature of consciousness, does not admit either a bifurcation, or a dichotomy, of subject and object within the ultimate reality. The implication of this metaphysical idealism is an epistemological idealism. It is now a short step to the conclusion that knowledge, which is constructed by subject and object, is illusive. Thus both the Mādhyamika and the Yogācāra reject the notion of relation and advocate a pure identity *(tādātmya)* of the ultimate reality with itself.

Yet another school that is opposed to the notion of relation, for the sake of revaluing the ultimate absolute reality, is Advaita Vedānta. Treatment of the Vedāntic school is of paramount importance to me, since Rāmānuja too belongs to a Vedāntic school. Since I shall devote my next chapter entirely to a critique of the critique of relation with reference to Advaita, here I shall be very brief, and very general too, in the exposition of the book.

Regarding the nature of the reality, Advaita Vedānta too holds similar view with that of the Buddhists. To it too, the ultimate reality is non-relational. Nonetheless, it is neither the 'nihilism' of the Mādhyamika nor the absolute idealism of the Yogācāra that we encounter here. For Advaitins are epistemologically realists, but metaphysically transcendentalists. Hence, their views deserve a closer attention.

Advaitin interprets the relational consciousness, whether internal or external, as the working of ignorance. This working impresses the empirical mind that makes knowledge of the external world possible. But this knowledge can not give us access to the nature of Brahman, the ultimate reality, which is relationless; it is a pure consciousness, distinct from any relational consciousness. In his commentary on the *Brahma-sūtra*, Śaṃkara, for example, criticises Nyāya relation of inherence (*samavāya*). Because *samavāya* is said to be an independent category, and because it relates two concepts, namely the substance and the attributes, it is objected to by Advaitin. It is asked, when *samavāya* establishes the relation between the two terms: how is it itself related to each of the terms that it relates?

How do we become aware of this relation that exists between the substance and *samavāya*, on the one hand, and between the attribute and *samavāya*, on the other? To account for these, we will be compelled to accept other *samavāya* relation. But this process of relating the relata will only lead us to an *infinite regress (anavasthā),* thus at once, demonstrating the self-contradiction, riddled with the relation of inherence. Hence, this fallacy of infinite regress led the Vedāntins to reject *samavāya* relation altogether as an entity, or category, standing independent of substance and attributes.

It is the inherent self-contradiction within the concept of relation that has led the Advaitins to institute the relation of *tādātmya* or *svarūpa*, in place of *samavāya*. The relation between the whole and the parts has been described by the Advaitins as a case of *tādātmya;* the analogy is further expanded to explicate the relation between Brahman, the relationless ultimate, and its illusory appearance as the world and its non-difference from the self. The 'realities' of the self and the world have been regarded by them as being identical with that of Brahman, even as the reality of the part is identical with that of the whole. The force of the argument of the Advaitins rests on this that the Nyāya-Vaiśeṣika systems cannot fully explain the real nature of the substance and attributes, and of their relation, when the latter admit *samavāya* to be a third category. Because the idea of substance cannot exist apart from that of the attributes, even as the idea of the attributes cannot equally exist apart from substance, Nyāya is said to commit the fallacy of mutual dependence *anyonyāśraya*. Nyāya has failed to demonstrate the clear-cut distinction between the two. They are inseparable both in our experience and in point of their existence; they may therefore be considered as the two aspects of the same entity. Substance expresses itself in attributes, and the attributes have their perfection and consummation in the substance. The two are identical in essence. Attributes exist when the substance is there; likewise they lack existence, when the substance is not there. Hence, there is no special relation between the two, they are identical *(tādātmya)*. Nyāya is mistaken in having invented a relation of inherence between the two. Therefore, the relation between the substance and attribute, between universal and particular etc. is said to be one of identity *(tādātmya),* if at all it can be called a relation. This searching analysis is fully employed by Advaitin to revalue Brahman's ultimacy as against its illusory manifestation as the world of selves and objects. By criticising *samavāya* relation, Advaitin shows that relations are unreal; that they hold good only for the empirical world. It is unable to grasp the transcendental reality, which is non-relational and which is ultimately real; the Absolute is supra-relational.

So far we have seen that the substantive-attributive relation, or the subject-object relation, has been rejected both by the Mādhyamika and the Yogācāra Buddhists and the Advaita Vedāntins. This is in part due to their negative and positive understanding of the nature of the reality respectively. Whereas, to the Buddhists, the absolute reality is so intensely negative that nothing can be attributed to it, to the Advaitin, it is so intensely positive that nothing can be attributed to it. Hence, both settle down to the view that reality is non-relational; and the relational appearance thereof are only for the illusory part of the human mind; it is due to illusion that reality appears as relational. In contradistinction to this view, the substantive-attributive relation is central to both Nyāya and Rāmānuja's philosophy. This is in part due to their realistic metaphysics; there is little wonder then that all the realists have accepted this relation in one form or another.

Despite the acceptance of the substantive-attributive relation, the meanings of Naiyāyika and Rāmānuja are here different. Naiyāyika is a *tārkika*, a logician *par excellence.* He arrives, by way of his logical analysis, to subscribe to his metaphysics of seven categories. Inherence *(samavāya)* is one and unique type of relation that is necessitated by, and to, his logical analysis. Given his definition of substance *(dravya)*, and such other categories as activity, quality etc., an independent category of inherence *(samavāya)* cannot but be posited; otherwise the categories would be hanging in the vacuum, and that hardly behooves his realism. But Rāmānuja in positing his *apṛthaksiddhi-bhāva* is more of an exegete than a logician; although he does possess considerable amount of logical acumen. As a Vedāntic exegete, he begins with Brahman as the concretely given, and with the world of selves and non-conscient matter as equally given within Brahman. The question then that he is faced with is: What is the relation between Brahman, *cit* and *acit*? His positing of the substantive-attributive relation is in the service of a Vedāntic hermeneutics. As I have mentioned earlier, Rāmānuja's Absolute is relational, because his conception of the Absolute is that of the concrete individual. If the ultimate reality is a concrete individual, it is not above the relational understanding. The relation which holds between Brahman and *cit,* on the one hand, and Brahman and *acit*, on the other, is an inseparable relation *(apṛthaksiddhi-bhāva)*. Needless to say, it is a type of substantive-attributive relation. It is an inner, inseparable, vital and organic relation, which holds between substance and its attributes.

We may now do well to compare Rāmānuja's substantive-attributive relation, that goes by the name of *apṛthaksiddhi-bhāva*, with the substantive-attributive relation of Nyāya that goes by the name of inherence *(samavāya)*.

Apṛthaksiddhi of Rāmānuja is similar to the *samavāya* of Nyāya in regard to its recognition of the reality, mutual necessity and the distinctiveness of the relata in it. Although to Nyāya *dravyas* are many, and they admit many attributes, to Rāmānuja, the ultimate reality is one indeed, in a sense non-dual, a supreme transcendental *dravya*, but with *cit* and *acit* as its attributes, more precisely, the modes *(prakāra)*. All the terms are here real and distinct, yet inseparable from one another. But there are differences between *samavāya* of Nyāya and *apṛthaksiddhi* of Rāmānuja, that must not be played down.

Firstly, unlike *samavāya, apṛthaksiddhi* is not a separate entity or a category, external to the relata. *Samavāya* is what relates substance and attribute as an external link; not so *apṛthaksiddhi-bhāva;* it is intrinsic to the terms related, apart from the relata, it has no separate existence. Secondly, the relata in *samavāya* remain mutually external, although they are held together in an 'extrinsic' unity by *samavāya.* It is because of the fact that *samavāya* is a relation in virtue of its being a category. In order that *samavāya* may hold good, there should be two genuinely different entities. But *apṛthaksiddhi* relation is not only an intrinsic relation, but also an organic one. It rejects both identity and difference. The relation at point is obtained in the inner relatedness of one and the same substance that admits within itself an internal differentiation. Thirdly, it follows from what we have suggested above that, whereas, to the Naiyāyikas, *samavāya*, being an 'external' and independent relation, is perceptible to senses, *apṛthak-siddhi* relation, to Rāmānuja,being internal to the relata, is not perceptible to the senses. The type of difficulty, that Naiyāyika faces in respect of the senses involved in the perception of *samavāya,* is clearly obviated by Rāmānuja in considering *apṛthak-siddhi* to be an internal and organic relation between the relata. Naiyāyika,for all his epistemological and logical acumen, is forced here to have recourse to an extra epistemological tool viz. *alaukika pratyakṣa* in the perception of the category of inherence. Rāmānuja however has no difficulty in this respect, precisely because *apṛthak-siddhi* relation is not an item for perception. After all, being a Vedāntin, he repudiates radical realism, and in this case it has been to his own advantage. Fourthly, *samavāya* is a relation merely between material substance and its attributes, while *apṛthaksiddhi* is a relation between immaterial substance Brahman and its attributes, both immaterial and material respectively. The perspective here is not that of a material substance as it is in Nyāya but that of the transcendental substance of Brahman.

Finally, *samavāya* is a necessary relation for only one of the relata. Thus the red colour that inheres in the rose can not but be in the substance rose, if it ever exists. The reversal of this relation is not necessary. Rose could be red, but it need not be so. The dependence of the rose on the red colour is contingent, but that of red colour in the rose is necessary. Not so, when we come to the internal organic relation of *apṛthaksiddhattva*. The terms here are mutually dependent, whereas *cit* and *acit* are entirely dependent on Brahman; Brahman receives his concrete individuality only through, and in, his modes of *cit* and *acit*. Some of the implications of this statement will be drastic, and I do hope to address myself to them, when I come to analyse the application of this relation in Rāmānuja's philosophy. Here, it is sufficient to state that *apṛthak-siddhi* is parallel to *samavāya* but, by no means, identical with it.

References

1. M. Hiriyanna, *The Essentials of Indian Philosophy,* George Allen & Unwin India Pvt. Ltd., 1949, p. 177.
2. V.S. Apte, *Sanskrit-English Dictionary*, Motilal Banarasidass, 1975.
3. Not in the Kantian but in an absolutistic sense.

3

Critique of Relation: A Critique

In previous chapter, in the context of setting *apṛthak-siddhi-bhāva* within a philosophy of relation in Indian philosophy, I very briefly touched upon the analysis of relation at the hands of Advaitin. The upshot of Advaitin's argument, determined as it is by his theory of reality, is that the concept of relation is riddled with contradictions. For relation is not possible without difference *(bheda)*; but all difference is, in the final analysis, meaningless within a non-dualistic framework. In this chapter, I would like to probe in depth into the central thesis of Advaita for the sake of bringing out how Rāmānuja subjects it to a critique of his own. Such a critique of the critique of relation is necessary for Rāmānuja's realistic and pluralistic epistemology, and to some extent, to his metaphysics as well. The upshot of Rāmānuja's critique, again, determined as it is by his theory of reality, is that the pure identity advocated by Advaitin comes to be a pure nothing. For the very talk about identity is made possible only through the concept of difference. If philosophy is not to discountenance our experience, difference is what is given in our experience. Its rejection therefore would be fraught with contradictions in our philosophical enterprise. More importantly, to Rāmānuja, the Vēdantic philosopher that he is, if we do not admit an internal differentiation *(svagata-bheda)* within Brahman, all knowledge of Brahman, and thereupon a Vedāntic metaphysics, should prove to be impossible.

We may begin here with an exposition of Advaita's critique of relation. Advaita claims to be a philosophy that is at once an intuition of reality. How is this intuition related to the phenomenon of knowledge, the more so, because every Vedāntin believes that knowledge is in the service of our understanding of reality? Knowledge in Advaita Vedānta is held to be both self-luminous and self-valid: it reveals its own existence as soon as it is born, and is not lighted up by any other illuminating factor. Its self-luminosity is referred to as an auto-illumination, *(svaprakāśatva)*, hence its existence is ever known *(jñātasattaka)*. Further, its validity too is guaranteed by the factors which bring about knowledge; no extraneous factors are ever required to ascertain its validity *(svataḥ-prāmāṇyatva)*. Hence Advaitin argues that the intuition of the ultimate reality is the absolute knowledge; it can only be of the nature of immediate experience; such an immediate experience of the ultimate reality is possible because the ultimate reality is pure-consciousness; its knowledge is not the one characterized by the duality of subject and object, but transcendental without a division in the consciousness.

Accordingly, Advaitin believes that Brahman, the transcendental reality, is an undifferentiated whole, an undifferentiated consciousness (*nirviśeṣa-cinmātra)*. It is one and unitary in its reality; it simply is, and can not be described as such and such; in short, it transcends or sublates all relational thought. Following closely certain trends in the *upaniṣads,* Advaitin thinks that Brahman should be conceived as acosmic (*niṣprapañca)*. Its reality is not essentially related to any thing other than itself, within or without. Brahman is thus regarded as the 'wholly non-dual' or the 'wholly one', to which nothing belonging to the world can be strictly predicated of.

In a sense, what the philosophers of religion speak of as the 'wholly other' pre-eminently suits Advaitic metaphysics, although Advaitin would find it repugnant to speak of any language of the 'other'. This non-predication of anything positive to Brahman is illustrated in the negative description of Brahman as 'not this, not this' *(neti-neti)*. Therefore Brahman is devoid of all determinations. It is pure being, consciousness and bliss *(sat-cit-ānanda)*, not in the adjectival sense, lest they may be mistaken for attributes of Brahman, but as experienced by the realized person. Therefore, Brahman is not an object of knowledge, rather it is pure knowledge itself. There is no knowing Brahman, rather there is only being Brahman. There is nothing beside, outside or within it. It cannot be described in terms of anything other than itself, because it does not enter into any relational process of knowledge. Brahman intuition is not a cognition in the form of a subject and object relation. It can only be known in a non-relational form.

It now goes without saying that criticism of relational understanding of reality is not merely a corollary of a non-dualistic metaphysics, as many Advaitins imagine, it is also one of the presupposition of the same metaphysics. We could even say that it occupies a central importance in Advaita philosophy. It is but natural, if Advaitin thinks that the supra-relational rests on the validity of this criticism of relation. What does Advaitin means by supra-relational absolute? He means by it positively a unity transcending all differences; negatively, it is a denial of the ultimacy of all relational forms of experience, as applied to the Absolute. Relations are true only for the empirical world but, from the metaphysical point of view, they are unreal: they do not hold good in respect of the ultimate, of final, reality. By implication, relations cannot give us any metaphysical truth, but only practical epistemic truths that have no final metaphysical significance.

Relational experience of reality is seen to be self-contradictory, because it is an attempt to take as diverse and plural what is fundamentally one. In relational experience, terms and relations that relate the terms must be taken to be different from, and outside of, one another; their unity, if ever posited, is unintelligible at the relational level. Relational experience of the ultimate must hence in its very nature be called self-contradictory, because the ultimate would not come under the purview of any relations.[1] For Advaita, non-contradiction *(abādhitatva)* is one of the criteria of truth, and accordingly, relational experience, which is self-contradictory in nature, cannot be the criterion of truth. Advaitin, in fact, goes to the extent of arguing that relational experience is not only self-contradictory in its essence, but also self-discrepant with the terms employed, and, in the end, indefensible. Therefore, they take relation to be neither primary nor ultimate in a metaphysical enterprise. Relational experience must fail in the end, if we ever employ it with the hope of reaching full reality, or truth.

To be fair to Advaita, it must be acknowledged that he does admit the concept of relation at the level of empirical knowledge of the world. But he refuses to give it any significance when it comes to the intuition of the transcendental reality. Indeed, relational experience, he thinks, is a development, or abstraction, from a non-relational felt-whole. The latter is its basis, or pre-condition, of the former. The former should consummate again in the non-relational experience, where its inner contradictions are resolved. Therefore, the essential pre-supposition and support of the relational experience remains throughout as the infra-relational, and the latter must give way once the higher state of identity, that transcends all relation, is reached. But, it is the trans-empirical immediate experience which is the foundation of all relational consciousness. The former is the measure of the latter and nor *vice versa*.

It is against this backdrop that we have to understand Śaṁkara's contention that the subject-object implications of knowledge can neither establish nor reveal truth. For truth is abiding, it cannot be established by relational, or pragmatic, consciousness, which after all only indulges in the constructions of a realistic will.

Śaṁkara's criticism of relations has been ably supported by Śrī Harṣa, a post-Śaṁkarite Advaita dialectician belonging to the eleventh century A.D. True to his task of employing the logical tools in the service of metaphysics, he takes up what may be regarded as the most general of all relations, namely the subject-object relation in knowledge for an analysis. He argues that we cannot maintain the reality of this relation independently of the terms it relates; indeed, no such relation intervenes between the subject and the object. For, if we maintain that a relation does intervene between the two, then, we are obliged to concede that it has an independent existence. In that case it would require another relation to connect the first relation with the terms of subject as well as the object. We would now be compelled to posit two more relations having independent existence. These in their turn would further require other relations to relate their own terms. The process thus leads us to a *regressus ad infinitum*. There is thus no subject-object relation at all, as distinguishable from the nature of the subject or the object in empiric epistemology. Indeed, the relation of subject and object is the essence of empiric epistemology, and the ground of concrete knowledge. But the Absolute, which is undifferentiated consciousness, does not connote any subject-object relation in its construction; we must not introduce here any dichotomy in consciousness. For relation is something 'mysterious', which can only give us appearance and not truth.

Brahman, to the Advaitin, is the perfect being, with no trace of any becoming. All becoming is symptomatic of imperfections inherent. Hence, all the categories of finite relational knowledge are applicable only to the universe which is finite or determinate. What is more, the absolutely real Brahman would lose its self-hood, if it ever were to become an object of relational knowledge. For that very reason Brahman does not admit of any substance-attribute relation which is the characteristic mark of all empirical knowledge. Likewise Brahman does not also admit of the kind of relation obtained between the part and whole; it is spoken of as the impartite *(akhaṇḍa)*.

Advaitin is thus led to hold the view that truth cannot be understood, it can only be 'seen' or intuited. A vision, or intuition, of truth is none other than reality in the completest and most perfect form, *ens realissimum*, to use the language of the Aristotelian Schoolmen. Advaita denies relation on the ground that, if there should be relation *(bhāva),* then there will also be difference *(bheda)*. This has serious implication to Advaita philosophy, for relational consciousness presupposes a differentiated consciousness too. To Advaita all *bheda-bhāva* refers to the truths of empiricality *(vyāvahārika-sattā)*, whereas the denial thereof refers to the transcendental truth of non-dualism *(pāramārthika-sattā)*. Advaitin therefore has recourse to scriptures on the point at issue. He avers that those scriptural statements *(śṛti-vākya)*, which deny difference *(bheda-niṣedha-śruti)*, establish non-difference *(abheda)*, and show that difference *(bheda)* is not ultimately real and has only phenomenal reality *(nehā-nenāsti-kiñcana)*. The innate obscuration of pure consciousness comes somehow to divide the absolute and to distort it into the world of difference. Difference *(dvirūpa)* cannot exist by itself; it is only a distortion of reality, because Brahman is relationless, therefore differenceless. He is a 'noumenon' as it were. Therefore Advaitin is led to assert that Brahman alone is, and what is not Brahman is 'false', as it is non-different from

Brahman even as the 'false' snake is non-different from the rope in the celebrated Advaitic rope-snake illusion.

Advaitin builds on this original intuition of the relationless, differenceless Brahman. Brahman is not only without any difference *(bheda)* but he is also without any activity, or movement *(niṣkriya)*, without any parts *(niravayava),* unconditioned and absolute *(nirupādhika)* and having no distinguishing element in it, a simple homogeneous entity *(nirviśeṣa)*. Brahman is one indivisible *(ekam, akhaṇḍa)*. In short, Brahman does not admit within itself any difference *(bheda)*, either *sajātīya, vijātīya* or *svagata*. These are the differences that obtain between the like-entities; alike-entities; and the internal differentiations within a single entity. Thus all differences are denied in the absolute unity. Advaita finds no room for the many in the unity of the pure non-differentiated entity that is Brahman. If there is the 'many' we would be forced to posit relation and, ultimately, there would be an endless multiplication of relations. Further, if there is relation, and the multiplication thereof, we would be forced to posit some difference; and thereby the unity of Brahman as the homogeneous reality cannot be established. Thus, the conception of unity embracing even a resemblance of difference of any type seems to be a hopeless one.

We must not miss here the significance of Advaitin's insistence on the character of metaphysical truth as distinct from epistemic truth lest we fail to grasp his distinction between intuition and knowledge by way of modification of consciousness. A truth which is related to subject cannot be the metaphysical truth according to Advaitin, for truth is abiding, eternal, all-pervasive and non-contradictory; it is what it is by its own nature; it should have no reference whatsoever to any conscious subject. Such a referenceless truth is the Reality that is Brahman, at once undivided. Divisions of existence in different grades do not correspond to it, they only correspond to the different epistemic forms of knowledge. But the Existence, Being as such, is Brahman; the same existence appears as different according to different organs of apprehension, while in reality it is the same one differenceless unity of being. If it appears as divided, it is because of the principle of *māyā*. Thus, Advaita philosophy is in a sense an attempt to overthrow the divisions of existence and their empirical truths, and thereupon to establish the transcendence of being. The absolutistic philosophy that it arrives at is the conclusion that the absolute is the locus of existence, and that it does not admit the partiality of division. The truth is not the fragmented beings but the complete being, the absolute. Partial visions of absolute being cannot pass for the fullness of being; if ever a claim is made, it is error, in the sense of a seeming reality claiming to be the absolute being.

Nothing could be more unfair to Advaita than to ascribe to it the view that Advaita attempts merely a synthesis of the partial presentations of appearance and being. Reality is not a synthesis of all partial truths; the sum total of partial truths is not the Truth. On the contrary, Advaita may be said to insist on the complete denial of the partial truths. Advaitin is aware that their synthesis cannot present the reality as it is in itself. The absolute is not a synthesis, but a pure identity. It is this category of identity which is the basis of his refutation of all relations and the consequent differences. His Absolute is neither a system after Hegel, nor an organism after Spinoza, nor a substance after Aristotle. His logic is based on the concept of identity *(tādātmya)*. Hence, it may be suggested that Advaitin's thought that Brahman is the 'sameness' of reality cuts at the root of all dualisms, of mind and matter, world and spirit, subject and object etc. This in part explains why Advaita does not rest satisfied with a mere refutation of the category of difference, but proceeds to assert the sameness of the Being. For it is possible that those, who reject difference, make for a doctrine of identity-cum-difference *(bhedābheda)* within a concrete universal; not for Advaitin is the fascination of a concrete universal.

Maṇḍana Miśra,[2] an Advaitin of an unsurpassed logical acumen, has presented to us the untenability of the concept of difference. He thinks that the dialectic of difference is self-defeating insofar as it fails to be an intelligible concept. He likewise attacks the concept of identity-cum-difference school, and points out that this latter difference turns out to be a device for self-deception through insufficient analysis. Positively, he establishes that identity is the only intelligible concept.

Advaita is in a position to reject objectivity too, in virtue of its rejection of difference. He ingeniously shows how objectivity is a creation of difference. He argues that objectivity is self-contradictory, self-stultifying and, therefore false, because an object becomes an object to consciousness, as distinct from other objects. In other words, no object is conceivable as object except as different from other objects. Difference *(bheda)* thus enters into the very structure and meaning of an object *qua* object. But, if difference, as a category, is self-contradictory and a false appearance, the concept of objectivity too, that is based on difference, is self-contradictory, self-invalidating and false. Just as we land into an endless series of difference to explain one single difference, we land into endless objects to establish a single object. If so, objectivity is unintelligible without the idea of difference, and it too must be a false appearance that cannot qualify to be reality. Advaitin thus would conclude that an object of consciousness is other than consciousness; therefore, it is other than reality as such, it is only a false appearance of the reality of pure consciousness. Likewise objectivity, as sustained by the idea of difference, is equally self-contradictory and, therefore, a false appearance of the reality of pure consciousness.

Pure consciousness itself, however, Advaitin contends, is intrinsically indefinable, as being unknowable *(avedya)*; if it ever admits of distinctions as this or that particular acts of consciousness *(vṛtticaitanya)*, it is only because it gets falsely identified with objects other than itself, which however are only false appearances. Therefore Advaita is very careful in passing the judgement that all plurality in consciousness is conditional and superimposed *(kalpita)*, and thereupon in recommending the negation of all things and attributes in Brahman. Intuition transcends all limitation of empirical modifications of consciousness, only when 'knowledge' has reached its frontiers and the ken of the empirical logic has finally died out. Only when the philosophic consciousness has risen to be transcendent, the seeming truths of divided life completely vanish; for the transcendental truth does not stand in any relation to the order of appearances. From this level of existence, the partial truths are, not only practically but also theoretically, non-existent. Thus far Advaita on the critique of relation.

Let me now turn my attention to the critique of this critique. Within his theoretical framework, the Advaitin's position does indeed seem impregnable. What is more, the Advaitin brings in abundantly the logical and epistemological insights to prove his position. But is his framework free from assumptions that can philosophically be sustained? What has Rāmānuja to state here?

One of the assumptions of Advaita, that seems to us philosophically not defensible, is its distinction between the two realms of human experience: the transcendental and the empirical. The critics of relation, and more importantly, of difference, seem to be quite keen on maintaining the difference between the two realms of human experience, and introduce a dichotomy within the core of experience itself, with which all our philosophical enterprise should begin. What is more, the metaphysics of Advaita, I am afraid, cannot synthesis the transcendental truth and the relative truths, as the relative truths are required to be sublated ultimately in the transcendental height of existence. It is not enough to state that truth is not a matter of synthesis but of identity. The fact, that Advaita makes a distinction between the transcendental and empirical truths, cannot exonerate Advaitin from the responsibility of relating them both to human experience. On the contrary, Advaita does not find any continuity between the higher and the lower realm of human experience. How at all would he speak of them as higher and lower, if they are not referred to an unity of experience? The transcendental truth of *Advaita* is not only transcendental, in the sense that it stands above the immanent order of space and time; but also in the sense that the immanent order does not really exist. How then do we begin our philosophical enterprise with something that is non-existent? On the contrary, if it is even claimed that transcendent appears as the immanent under the sway of ignorance, and therefore the latter has no ultimate significance, how can it be the starting point of our philosophical enterprise in all earnestness and seriousness?

Rāmānuja has been quick to point out the above infelicities in Advaita. He has drawn therefore no distinction between the absolute and the relative truths, between absolute and relative knowledge, in the way Advaita does. However, he too accepts the latter distinction between the absolute and the relative knowledge in another way. To him, knowledge is relative, when it has not reached its fuller development and concreteness. In the same strain, knowledge is absolute when it has reached to the concreteness of Brahman. Thus knowledge of an aspect of reality is, no doubt, relative, if it is not seen in its totality; if the absolute knowledge is to emerge, all the relations, which knowledge implies, must be seen in a completely unified system. Thus to Rāmānuja a grandiose unity in Brahman is truth. Presentations of diversity in their isolation are imperfect presentation of truth, but they are by no means false, as they are to Advaita. Such a view of truth as a grandiose unity has serious implications to Rāmānuja's metaphysics in general and, to epistemology, in particular. For Advaita, as has been already shown, denied a unity of subject and object in a synthesis, as for as his absolute truth, or knowledge, is concerned. The epistemology of Advaitin, therefore, is true of relative consciousness but not of absolute consciousness that Brahman is. But the epistemology of Rāmānuja is true of absolute consciousness as well. This is because his categories of knowledge, understood as the attributive knowledge *(dharma-bhūta-jñāna)*, are applicable no less to Brahman than to the individual self. By its very nature, knowledge is relational.

For Rāmānuja, truth is a complete system. Our knowledge, which is necessarily relational, is to develop the complete system within itself; otherwise it suffers from a limitation and cannot be truth at all. Therefore metaphysics cannot remain satisfied without the whole network of knowledge spreading out in a system in its many relational aspects, and apprehending the parts in a synthesis of the whole. Since knowledge spreads out the network of relations, apprehends and synthesizes the parts of the whole, metaphysics is not immune to relations; metaphysics too spins out a relational scheme of all forms of knowledge, and tends to transcend division and partial presentations in a complete unity. Thus the impacting of metaphysics and epistemology is mutual. Further, since in Rāmānuja being is consciousness, the metaphysical theory cannot be disconsonant with those of epistemology; indeed, epistemology must present the complete development of knowledge in a unified system; at any rate, it must not be satisfied with the presentation of a partial aspect of the reality. All knowledge therefore must possess concreteness and definiteness, because definiteness strictly is the characteristic mark, or *differentia,* of knowledge. There cannot be an incohate knowledge. If it ever lacks its *differentia*, it ceases to be knowledge, it remains simple apprehension. One clearly perceives the difference here between Advaita and Rāmānuja: For Advaita truth is not a synthesis at all of all partial truths, but the complete denial of them. Hence its insistence on the absolute as identity. Not so for Rāmānuja. The truth is the definite absolute with all its multifarious relations that are synthesized within it harmoniously.

To be sure, it is a theistic presentation of knowledge and truth. It fundamentally differs from all monistic and non-dualistic presentation of knowledge and truth. The theistic endeavour in epistemology everywhere has been largely synthetic. Not for it is the sectional presentation of reality; likewise not for it is the complete transcendence of knowledge. For one thing, the theistic reality is all inclusive, admitting within itself all phases of being. The theist argues that reality must be complete and all inclusive, and all pervasive. The seeming appearance too, in virtue of the fact of seemingness, has a reality of its own and therefore must not be completely denied. For another, the seeming presentation has its own epistemological significance, as it too is an experience, calling for a meaningful epistemological explication; it is a noetic situation that bears upon a presentation. To uphold initially that there is a presentation and in the same breath to deny it thereafter is no explanation of any epistemic presentation. Finally, the complete denial of the presentation is also not a fact experienced by anyone. Therefore the theist with his concern for synthesis of experience refuses to make a distinction between being and presentation, for, to him, all presentations only report the being, and its modes. As such there can be no complete division eternally obtaining within truth; hence, if anybody denies the synthetic character of all presentations, it also must make all knowledge impossible.

Precisely at this stage Rāmānuja clinches the issue of relation as a necessity for any knowledge, as against Advaita to whom real can never be an object of knowledge. For Rāmānuja, on the contrary, there cannot be knowledge without a reference to real. Our knowledge is always concrete, and concrete knowledge has of necessity a reference to being. Knowledge and being are mutually inclusive, in the sense that, knowledge is always of the being, even as being is known to be a concrete being only through knowledge. In virtue of its being concrete, its tendency is to reveal itself in its complete nature; therefore every knowledge expresses its own object. Therefore, every knowledge has a reference to an object; an objectless knowledge, in the sense of being free from its object, is a chimera. It now follows for Rāmānuja that, if the determination of knowledge is by its object, it can never be conceived as transcending relations. Relations constitute the warp and woof of a cognitive act. In short, knowledge is essentially relational consciousness, and this relational consciousness cannot be totally false. All this goes to indicate the importance given by Rāmānuja to subject the Advaitin's critique of relation to a reverse critique, and thus to establish the truth that relation occupies a central place in his metaphysics.

Rāmānuja criticises the Advaitin that the latter's understanding of a relationless Absolute, precisely because of its being devoid of all relations, makes for an abstract and, not a concrete entity. It makes for an exclusive principle of rigid identity. Moreover, it fails to reconcile the unity with multiplicity, nay more, it ends up negating the latter to revalue the former. But, Rāmānuja asserts, reality is too rich and complex to be confined within the narrow limits of rigid identity. And his contention here is not without reasons.

A relation implies that two terms, which may be said to have been once apart from each other, are now held together. Relation therefore is the cementing bond between the two terms, while the nature of relation itself consists in its force of binding the realities; and it thus makes for unity of realities with its presence or for diversity with its absence. Rāmānuja argues that neither unity nor diversity sums up the nature of a real; the nature of the real is constituted by both taken together. Hence he thinks that the denial of relations would in fact reduce all things to nullity. Even the ineffable reality would not be an exception to its being apprehended, if not fully comprehended, by way of its attributes; hence, the determination by way of relations is the structure of reality. Therefore an existent, having no determination, is a fiction; so, the negations of determinations make for the negation of reality itself. Moreover, Rāmānuja contends that relation, whether internal or external, is integral to the terms. Such an integral relation is the result of an internal change in the nature of terms. The denial of relations, he believes, involves a self-contradiction, if for no other reason than that such a denial is possible only by virtue of relational thought. There is no thought that operates outside the scheme of relations.

Rāmānuja's critique of the critique of relation should not be seen merely negatively. For he positively thinks that the universe with its subjective and objective aspects is the result of a self-differentiation of the absolute. Both aspects serve as members of a relational system. The conscient *(cit)* and the inconscient *(acit)* are the finite modes of the Absolute, and have no independent existence, apart from that of the Absolute Brahman. They are internally related with Brahman. It is here that Advaitin's logic seems to have gone astray, according to Rāmānuja. Since the relation of the modes of *cit* and *acit* with Brahman is internal, and not external, it will not lead to *regressus ad infinitum,* as Advaitin would argue. Thus

Rāmānuja attributes to the supreme reality an internal variegatedness, that at once make for the internal unity of the inanimate and the animate entities within the supreme reality itself. The supreme is thought of as having an inward dispersion, a self-differentiation, within itself by an internal necessity; the internal necessity, because it follows from its own will, does not suggest any sense of unfulfilled purposes within the absolute, lest one should think of a pure spontaneity as determined by external goals.

We should carefully take note of what Rāmānuja has done here lest we should accuse Rāmānuja of abjuring his Vedāntic tradition. On the contrary, he is a Vedāntin to the fullest sense. For, to him, Brahman is the sole reality, in the sense that outside, or independent, of Him there is nothing else. Brahman is devoid of the two kinds of external distinctions. They are the external distinctions between the two unlike entities *(vijātīya-bheda),* and between two like entities *(sajātīya-bheda)*. While the former asserts both unity and the absolute sovereignty of Brahman, and thereby negates any type of crass dualism, the latter asserts the uniqueness of Brahman and negates any type of crass pluralism at the metaphysical level and crass polytheism at the religious level. But, in contradistinction with Śaṁkara. Rāmānuja admits an internal distinction *(svagata-bheda)* within Brahman. For there are within Brahman the different conscious and unconscious substances; and they can be not only mutually distinguished but also distinguished from Brahman. This internal relation is both natural *(svābhāvika)* and eternal *(sanātana)*.

It however needs to be shown that Rāmānuja, far from abjuring his Vedāntic tradition, is deeply rooted in it. Reality, to Rāmānuja too, is the non-dual spirit *(advaya)*. But it is not a distinctionless homogeneous identity *(nirviśeṣa-tādātmya),* as it is to Advaita. Although it may be true that every judgement may be said to affirm identity, we must not forget here another equally important factor, namely difference. Indeed, the principles of identity and contradiction (in this case of difference) go together because they are the two aspects of the same reality. This is because of the nature of thought process itself. Thought qualifies reality that it aims to apprehend congnitively or affectively. Thought presupposes a distinction between subject and object, but the distinctions, having been recognized as distinctions, are also integrally united, and not kept on isolated bits in the process of apprehending. Therefore, the ultimate reality cannot be a bare undifferentiated unity, but a unity that contains, and admits as such, differences which are all real. All determinations, limitation and differences are deep within the heart of it. They are also not left unorganised, but they are harmoniously coordinated. Further the differences, which are accommodated and harmoniously coordinated in this unifying principle, do not vanish at any time. It is not the case that the differences within reality are entertained only for a while and then relegated to oblivion as of no ultimate significance. Rather they are co-eval and co-eternal with the unity of the reality, even though we may say that they are subject to change from subtle to gross state in the process of evolution *(sṛṣṭi),* and from the gross to the subtle state in the process of involution *(pralaya)*.

Rāmānuja's Absolute then is a concrete individual. If we ever speak of it in terms of identity at all, it is an identity in the sense of unity, achieved in and through difference; it is an identity impregnated with differences. Thus, a relation of difference is the pivot on which his philosophy revolves. Pure identity, or bare being, of Brahman without any differentiation, is a metaphysical fiction; it has no adequacy in perceptual experience, which by its nature is relational experience. If we have referred here to perception, it is because it is the basis of all other forms of knowledge. We could as well say that all knowledge involves discrimination, and it is impossible to know an undifferentiated object; all knowledge is in and through difference. Likewise all unity is in and through, and because of, diversity, that makes at once a pure identity into a pure nothing. True to his Vedāntic spirit, Rāmānuja bases his argument for the impossibility of an undifferentiated reality on *tarka, śṛti* and *smṛti*. An undifferentiated reality cannot even be proved to exist, because all proofs are based on the assumption that the *probandum* is of some qualified character. There cannot be a proof of an undifferentiated substance in our experience. Neither *śabda* nor perception nor inference can prove the existence of an unqaulified substance. Likewise neither *śṛti* nor *smṛti* has ever proved its existence. In short, while, speaking negatively, there is no proof anywhere of a substance devoid of all difference, speaking positively, the only real revealed by the means of knowledge, *śṛti* and *smṛti* is one characterized by difference. Therefore Advaitin's contention that all differences, therefore, all relations, are ultimately unreal, stands *eo ipso* refuted.

In virtue of the establishment of the relational character of all knowledge, Rāmānuja is in a position to argue out that Brahman as pure thought is false. On the contrary, Brahman, the supreme being, may be conceived as self, or person, or possessed of auspicious qualities because it is, as a concrete real, characterized by differences. Indeed, everything experienced is found to display differences within itself; therefore all proof cannot but rest on experience. It is against this rock of experience, that is, by its nature relational, that all Advaitic arguments for an undifferentiated pure thinking should flounder. For, if Advaitin ever attempts to prove it, it will begin to display attributes; anything that is capable of being proven must have attributes. If, on the other hand, Advaitin does not care to prove it, it is reduced to a mere fanciful hypothesis, an abstraction, contradicted by experience. There cannot be a pure thinking but only thinking qualified by thought. Therefore Brahman cannot be either a qualityless Being or a pure thinking. Brahman ought to be a self characterized by thought as well as by several other attributes. It is for the same reason that Brahman cannot be regarded as pure unity; it ought rather to be a unity that includes within itself differences. A concrete real cannot but be an unity of a plurality of aspects and modes, therefore a unity and diversity in one.

Precisely because Rāmānuja makes his philosophy a philosophy of relations, he is in a better position than any Advaitin to solve the perennial philosophical problem of the one and the many. He safeguards both one and many, true to the spirit of a healthy realism, without denying the many for the sake of affirming the one, and also without denying the one for the sake of affirming the many. This is not a rejection of the Vedantic tradition, because he makes the many the predicate of the one. Thus we see that the problem of the one and the many is seen by Rāmānuja, not in their opposition, but in their marvellous complementarity. Hence his metaphysics is non-dualistic without ceasing to be either realistic or pluralistic. The unique relation of difference, unity and mutuality between Brahman *cit* and *acit* is *apṛthak-siddhi* relation. Needless to say, in order to speak of this relation, Rāmānuja had to argue for the concept of relation itself against the Advaitin. The fuller implications of the justification comes to him from his conception of Brahman as the living reality with a creative urge. While Advaitin would be averse to speak of any synthesis in Brahman, Rāmānuja has no hesitation to speak of Brahman as a synthesis which does not deny differentiations; rather Brahman expresses itself through its differentiation only: Brahman is a totality without negating its parts; it is a substance without negating its attributes; it is a ground without negating its consequent; it is an integrity without negating all that makes for its integralness. Within its concrete being contain all the finite, as though the latter are the moments of its own existence. What is more, the finite is not a mere embellishment to the Infinite, for through them the latter transcends its own abstract character. Thus, to Rāmānuja, reality is a complex whole that at once includes both unity and diversity, the oneness and the manyness, without destroying its own unicity or uniqueness.

The diversity of manyness constitutes the modes of Brahman's all inclusive reality. The modes are different from Brahman, yet they do not create any division within the integralness of his being, as Brahman is said to realise its synthetic character through the modes. The latter, on their part, do not have a distinctive existence of their own, they rather make for the 'adjectives', or modes, of the former, thus vouching for the fact that they cannot be understood without reference to Brahman, their substance. The mutuality then between the substance and the modes is complete without any contradiction between the unity and the plurality. Both are safeguarded by *apṛthak-siddhi* relation. Rāmānuja's rejection of an absolutistic principle of bare identity and the affirmation of a living principle of differentiation at the very heart of identity are made possible on the basis of *samānādhi-karaṇya*. The principle of *samānādhi-karaṇya* makes for the co-existence of unity and diversity and their intimate relation to each other. The two are distinct and, yet not contradictories, and they can be reconciled in a synthetic unity.

It may be of some interest for us here to note that the acceptance or the rejection of the concept of difference introduces not only different approaches to reality but also different modes of thinking itself. The principal law of thinking to Advaitin is the law of identity, which in its strict application, would read as 'being is being'. In its contradictory aspect, now, being and non-being are mutually exclusive. Since Brahman alone is real, everything that is thought to be real must be 'false' or non-being. Therefore the being that is asserted is itself without any other being within or without. Rāmānuja, on the contrary, would have nothing against a principal law of thinking as identity, but it is not a bare identity. It is an identity that does not cancel within itself distinctions. It is not the contradiction of being and non-being that Rāmānuja is interested in; it is rather the unity of being in which the oppositions or distinctions are assimilated. He would admit within the dialectics of thought the overcoming of thesis and antithesis in an organic unity, yet not as Hegel would think. Rāmānuja thinks that it is the tendency of thought to move from abstract to concrete; therefore thought is to make the bare indeterminate cognition into determinate and concrete. Rāmānuja therefore assigns the thought the tasks of building up a concrete world of knowledge, in which all the parts are unified in a system. In asserting the principal law of thought as unity (not so much identity), while he is different from Advaitin, he is also different from Hegel, insofar as he refuses to recognize *contradiction* as a law of thought, so very vital to the Hegelian dialectics. Rāmānuja would contend that thought thinks in distinctions, and not in contradictions. The necessity of thought is to build up a unity of system, and in that system parts are seen in the whole both in their identity and distinctions. Therefore when we perceive the whole, we perceive a synthesized identity of existence; therefore it is not an abstract but concrete identity.

Our reference to the Hegelian system, casual though, is an occasion here for us to point out the distinctive character of Rāmānuja's metaphysics of relations. While his metaphysics, is, in a sense, the non-dualistic Vedānta, yet it makes for a qualified non-dualism, as against Advaitin. Likewise it makes for an organismic non-dualism, as against Hegel. Hence, his philosophy should be conceived after the analogy of an organism, involving internal differentiations, rather than a relationless entity, or an abstract spirit, that evolves due to an inner force. His philosophy, as a true system of thought, recognises both the distinctive elements of the one and the many, and yet rises above them to a higher principle, a synthesis in which all distinctions are reconciled; in his conception of being with internal differentiation, unity and diversity, or plurality, are rolled into one. An organismic theory of being fulfils the task by way of admitting a unity, which expresses itself in and through the diversity of forms and functions. It is however important that we bear in mind here that an idea of a living organism is not that of a barren abstract unity bereft of multiplicity of its organs. It is rather a concrete unity, which realises itself in and through that multiplicity. Rāmānuja's merit consists in not merely asserting this concrete unity but in arguing it out logically, that has a bearing on his refutation of any rejection of the concept of relation. A part is not intelligible except through the idea of the whole, of which it is a part; coversely, a whole is not conceivable without any reference to its constituent parts. In the same way, the organs, that are the parts of the organism, are not intelligible except by the idea of the organism; conversely, the organism also is not conceivable without any reference to the organs, that are the parts of the organism. Thus, the concept of organism regards the one and the many as members of an organic whole: each has its own being, and yet intricately related to each other. Such a philosophy of unity of being with its own internal diversity would be unimaginable without safeguarding the crucial concept of relation. Rāmānuja fittingly spares no efforts to establish the validity of relation in philosophy.

References

1. Vimuktātman, a great exponent of Advaita, advances at the beginning of his work, *Iṣṭha-siddhī*, some arguments to show the enigmatic nature of the subject-object relation.
2. See his *Brahmasiddhi*.

4

Apṛthak-Siddhattva between Brahman and *Acit-Prapañca*

The relation, that holds good between Brahman on the one hand, and the objective world *(acit-prapañca)* as well as the subjective world *(cit-prapañca)* on the other, is called by Rāmānuja an inseparable relation *(apṛthak-siddhi-bhāva)*. In this chapter, I shall be concerned with the application of this relation of inseparability, partially: How does this relation hold good between Brahman and the objective world? I shall also here devote my attention to some of the philosophical problems associated with this relation of the world *(jagat)* with Brahman. Rāmānuja does indeed take note of these problems and attempt to solve them within his own Vedāntic framework.

Surprisingly no Advaitin has found the need to criticise Rāmānuja's *apṛthak-siddhi-bhāva*. They all have taken it to be refuted, once the generic category of relation *(bhāva)* itself is refuted *(bheda-dhikkāra)*. What need is there now to refute a specific type of relation that goes by the name of inseparability? Advaitic thinkers that have come after Rāmānuja too have relied on their classical refutation of difference and relation. Rāmānuja however has subjected the Advaitic critique of relation, as shown in the previous chapter, and thereupon has consolidated on the application of his specific type of relation between Brahman, *cit* and *acit*. We can readily appreciate his concern that give special importance to the concept of inseparable relation *(apṛthak-siddhi-bhāva)* by insisting on his metaphysical truth that reality is a relational whole. It is a relational whole especially because it includes the world within itself as its mode, real and full-blooded entity. This necessarily brings him to a criticism of the Advaitin's theory of the world as 'illusion' *(māyā-vāda)*. He is of the view that, as the world is rooted in Brahman, it has as much, nay, the same, reality as Brahman; far from being an illusion, the world is a part of Brahman. Not only both *jagat* and Brahman are inseparably related to each other, but they are also mutually dependent on each other by the rule of *samānādhi-karaṇya*. This follows from the fact that reality is not a bare identity but a concrete unity wherein both the sameness and the difference co-exist and mingle with each other.

Of the three fundamental principles *(tattva-traya)* of his metaphysics, *acit* is the inconscient *(jaḍa)*. It corresponds to the unconscious matter *(prakṛti)*. Unlike the radical realists, Nyāya-Vaiśeṣika, Sāṁkhya-Yoga, or the radical pluralist Vedāntin like Madhva, Rāmānuja conceives of *prakṛti* to be a part of Brahman. But in making the imperfect inconscient *prakṛti* an integral part of the perfect and conscious Brahman, there arise a great many philosophical problems for Rāmānuja. What are these problems? How does Rāmānuja hope to solve them in his philosophy? We will see here carefully how crucial a role the relation of *apṛthak-siddhattva* plays both in the formulation of the problems and in their resolution in Rāmānuja's philosophy.

While it is generally true that Rāmānuja's Vedānta developed in direct opposition to Śaṁkara's Advaita, nowhere is his opposition stronger than where Rāmānuja discusses the relation of the world and the self with the Brahman. If we restrict ourselves to the former, here, a basic feature of his opposition is the downright rejection of Advaita's *māyā-vāda*, and here too, the Advaitin's understanding of *prakṛti,* the principle of the material world. Whereas the Advaitin regards the creative efforts of Brahman as only an apparent expression of the absolute under the conditions of *māyā,* Rāmānuja, on the other hand, regards it as a real transformation of *prakṛti,* which is a mode of Brahman. Therefore, while, to the Advaitin, the world is an illusory transformation *(vivarta),* to Rāmānuja, on the other hand, it is a genuine transformation *(pariṇāma)* of *prakṛti,* that exhibits at once the realistic attitude of Rāmānuja towards the universe. Nonetheless *prakṛti*, being a mode of Brahman, would seem in its transformations to affect also Brahman. Rāmānuja does not fight shy of the philosophical problem here. He fully falls back upon his Vedānta to make of Brahman not only the efficient cause *(nimitta-kāraṇa)* but also the material cause *(upādāna-kāraṇa)* of the world. To the philosophical infelicity itself I will return a little later.

Rāmānuja is led to think that, if Advaitin denies the significance of the cosmic process, it is because of his static concept of being. The denial of the cosmic process has brought about the dynamic concept of life and experience being totally overshadowed by the extreme transcendentalism of the static Absolute. For the static and eternally complete Absolute, by its very definition, admits of neither change nor transformation. Even if the Advaitin has introduced the category of the empiricality *(vyāvahārika-sattā),* or phenomenality *(prātibhāṣ ika)*, it only lays bare the limitation of any transcendental philosophy that hopes to thrive on the rejection of the world of life and experience. For the latter will have no intrinsic worth from the viewpoint of the absolute, that has robbed the world of its essential significance as a reality in its own right. Since the Advaitin's Brahman is of a absolute homogeneous nature, it is absolutely destitute of qualities.[1] But since Rāmānuja's, Brahman is neither homogenous nor devoid of qualities, Rāmānuja is in a position to acknowledge the intrinsic worth of the world, and incorporate it within his concept of the dynamic reality of Brahman.

The theory of reality advocated by Advaitin is dis-consonant with a theory of the reality of the world. After all, the world is the ground of all human experience; its rejection should be fraught with nihilating human experience itself. For if Brahman alone is real, how are we to account for our experience of the plurality of the universe? How can the world of manifold multiplicity arise from one unitary self? This is the vexed problem of the one and the many, faced by any metaphysics, but felt with all its severity in the transcendental philosophy of Advaita. Advaitin's own solution of the problem is that Brahman alone is real and the world of variegatedness is an illusory manifestation *(vivarta)* of Brahman, caused by *māyā* or *avidyā,* which is somehow positive and beginningless but an indescribable *(anirvacanīya)* phenomenon. In this solution Advaitin disvalues the reality of the world in order to revalue the reality of his transcendental principle. But Rāmānuja would ask, if it is necessary to exhibit the philosophical attitude of negating the world in order to affirm Brahman. What is more important, do we gain a solution to the problem of the one and the many? Rāmānuja thinks that the device of *māyā* is more a dialectical mystification of the problem than a genuine solution thereof. It is a *tertium quid*, an intermediary position, nonetheless a position for all the Advaitic protests, between being and non-being, *sat* and *asat*; and it aims at doing away with the contradiction resultant upon the conjunction of *sat* and *asat*. To be sure, the logic of dichotomy between being and non-being is riddled with contradiction that seeks to be resolved in our experience. But a resolution cannot be sought by way of doing away with the ground of experience itself viz. the world. Hence, Rāmānuja thinks that *māyā* is an evasive device which itself harbours the very contradictions it seeks to resolve. Even Advaitin may be said to acknowledge it, in a sense, by calling it a *sadasad-vilakṣaṇa*. Secondly, the existence and the reality of the world is a perceived fact and, in denying it's complete reality, Advaitin seems to be rejecting the very basis of the normal experience. Let it be noted here that it is not a case of our perceptual experience being immune from error; the case is rather of negating the sense of reality itself to the world, the object of our perceptual experience. The basis of a perceptual experience is not anything transcendental but the locus of that experience. Resolution of the problems that arise within the world of perceptual experience must be sought, not out of, but in, that world of perceptual experience. Thirdly, Advaitin's theory of the illusoriness of the world, brought about by the devise of *māyā-avidyā,* leads to an infinite regress: According to the Advaitin, *avidyā* is the cause of the illusory world, and this *avidyā* in itself is neither real nor unreal. Let us grant it for argument's sake that it is not real. If, on the other hand, *avidyā* is also not unreal, in order to account for the world process, we will be forced to give it at least a semblance of an 'active negativity'. Then, another active negativity would have to be postulated in order to account for the nature and activity of *avidyā.* But this process, we readily perceive, is never-ending. We have landed in the worst type of infinite regress, which only suggests the futility of divesting the world of experience of all reality.[2]

Not merely a philosopher but a Vedāntic hermeneutician and the high priest of a temple that he was, Rāmānuja contends that the theory of *avidyā* is not supported by either *śṛti,* or *smṛtis* or *purāṇas.* While it is true that *prakṛti* is in some texts spoken of in the above literature as *māyā*, the expression however does not mean *mithyā,* in the sense of unreality. While in the *Vedas* Indra is said to take on different forms by way of his power *(māyā),* the *purāṇas* have been explicit in stating that the weapons of *asuras* are made of *māyā.* In either case *māyā* does not mean unreal, rather it denotes the power that produces various wonderful effects. Viewed as the great power that effects real objects, *prakṛti* is the great womb of creation. It is the principle responsible for the variegated world and its process, as is amply evidenced by the *śṛti* texts.[3]

Rāmānuja therefore rejects outright the Advaitic account of a twofold reality as transcendental and empirical; and the consequent account of the noumenality of Brahman and the phenomenality of the world of experience. The rejection of these arbitrary distinction has made a unity of the world in Brahman feasible in his philosophy. A unity of Brahman is therefore in no way incompatible with the reality of the world.

Rāmānuja takes the Advaitin to task for divesting the world of all reality on the basis of the latter's concept of sublation. In doing this, Rāmānuja himself introduces a distinction between the Advaitic concept of sublation and that of non-persistence. He contends that the failure on the part of the Advaitin to make this distinction has led him to view the world of plurality as unreal. The concept of sublation makes for the rejection of one experience by another experience, on the ground that the former comes into conflict with the latter, which simply cancels the latter. In the light of the latter, the former is proved to be false. On the contrary, the concept of non-persistence makes for the position that an object may be non-persistent, in the sense that it exists only for a brief period of time; nevertheless, it is real in a true sense. There is no question of its either falsity or unreality. That an object exists only for a short time does not condemn it to the realm of unreality. Persistence for a while is the very character of the world-process, insofar as the manifest *prakṛti* in creation has the power to become un-manifest in dissolution. Becoming of the world is its nature, although all becoming takes place within the being of Brahman. Thus, Rāmānuja concludes that the Advaitin's attempt at relating the pure, non-differentiated Brahman to a world of plurality, by way of declaring the latter to be unreal, on the strength of sublation, through the category of beginningless *avidyā-māyā* is philosophically unwarranted and also self-defeating; besides it lacks all scriptural authority, too.• From this he concludes to his own thesis that the world with all its change and multiplicity is real; that there is no reason to call it either futile *(tuccha)* or false *(mithyā)*; that the cosmic evolution takes place in the being of Brahman; and that therefore it could also be said to be an aspect of the self-transformation of Brahman, insofar as *prakṛti* constitutes the *acit-prakāra* of Brahman.

Just as Rāmānuja rejects the notion of sublation in respect of the world of plurality, he also does not accept the distinction between the transcendence of consciousness and immanence of will in the creative effort of Brahman, as conceived by Advaitin. Reality cannot be so bifurcated; such a bifurcation of the reality into a transcendent consciousness and an immanent will opens up the dangerous philosophical game of ascribing all reality to the former, and divest it of the latter by making the world process a playful fabrication of will, that ultimately lacks all metaphysical significance. On the contrary, it is the one and the same Brahman, who is both immanent in the world as its inner controller, and transcendent to it as its ground and support. That Brahman is a unity of consciousness and will, that are at once transcendent and immanent, is the firm belief of Rāmānuja. Rāmānuja is quite clear in his mind that the world has its own status and individuality in and through Brahman. Brahman is not the world but he is the soul of the world. As the soul of the world, Brahman is the self 'hidden in all beings' and 'seen by suitable seers through their sharp and subtle intellect.'[4]

Rāmānuja depends on the scriptures, the true Vedāntin that he is, not only to refute Advaitin's view on the relation between the world and Brahman, but also to establish his own thesis of *apṛthak-siddhattva* between the two. He has recourse to the *upaniṣads,* and the *Gītā* in particular. In the opinion of Rāmānuja, the *upaniṣads* abundantly testify to the realistic nature of the world. And yet, they do not recognise a second principle, over and above, or side by side with, and independent from, Brahman, so that the second principle would be conceived of as the material necessary for creation. The picture of the world process therein is thought in terms of an emanation rather than a creation; nonetheless, far from rejecting the reality of the world, they affirm the world process in Brahman. Such views are amply expressed in such scriptural passages as:

> As a spider comes out with its thread, as small sparks come forth from fire, even so from this soul come forth all vital energies, all worlds, all gods, all beings.[5]

Again,

> I, indeed, am this world for I emitted it all from myself.[6]

Thus, the world is said to be the product of what originally was undifferentiated; the undifferentiated becomes differentiated by names and forms *(nāma-rūpa)*.[7] Creation of the world therefore is a 'sending forth' of the world by Brahman out of itself, rather than a production out of nothing as is the case with the Semitic tradition. Rāmānuja is deeply rooted in his Indian and Vedāntic heritage.

While subscribing to the evolutionary status of the world, on the basis of scriptures, Rāmānuja is not a deist; he is, unlike a non-dualist, a theistic Vedāntin. For though the world emanates out of Brahman, it does not fall apart from it at any stage of its existence. Both in its unmanifest and manifest forms, it is dependent on Brahman. What is more, Brahman is said to be immanent in his creation through and through. Even for this view, Rāmānuja once again has recourse to the scriptures. The *upaniṣads* repeatedly declare that, after creating the world, Brahman entered into it 'even to the finger nail tips'.[8]

Numerous are the passages in the *upaniṣads,* where the thoroughness of this immanence is emphatically declared.[9] One of the finest passages, on which Rāmānuja bases some of his arguments, is the following:

> He dwells in the earth, in the waters, in the fire, in the atmosphere, in the wind, in the sky, in the sun, in the quarters of heaven, in the moon and stars, in space, in the darkness, in the light, in all things.[10]

This passage is deliberately cited by me because a view, that the scriptural support to Rāmānuja does not come from the earlier *upaniṣads* but only from the so-called later theistic *upaniṣads,* has somehow gained ground in the history of Indian philosophy. Nothing could be far from the truth.

The *Gītā* is the representative text, to most Vedāntic thinkers, for *smṛti.* Rāmānuja's citing from this source is considerable for arguing out the essential dependence of the world on Brahman. Like most of the *upaniṣads*, it too teaches that the world forms a part of the supreme. It is created, supported and dissolved by him.[11] While accepting this general position of the *upaniṣads,* the *Gītā* also describes the process of 'creation' and dissolution; it enumerates the various elements involved in it. Rāmānuja sought support for the doctrine of repeated creations both from the *Gītā* and the *Śvetāśvatara Upaniṣad.*[12] His indebtedness to Sāṁkhya comes through the *Gītā,* insofar as Rāmānuja accepts the view that creation proceeds substantially through the stages depicted by the Sāṁkhya philosophy.

Finally, he also derived from the *Gītā* the idea that, in creating the world, Brahman is not prompted by any desire. His appellations to Brahman as *satya-kāmaḥ, satya-saṁkalpaḥ* are derived from the *Gītā* to highlight the truth that Brahman, in being the creator, is not characterized by any lack or imperfection in his nature.

Despite accepting *prakṛti* in its nature as an uncreated eternal reality *(aja)* and as the principle of creation, and also the manner of its creation, after Sāṁkhya philosophy, Rāmānuja is quick to distinguish *prakṛti* from its Sāṁkhya counterpart. He reiterates that *prakṛti* is a part of Brahman, and is controlled by Brahman, just as the human body is controlled from within by the human soul. In the state of dissolution *(pralaya)* of the world, its principle, the primal inconscient nature of *prakṛti* remains in a latent, subtle *(sūkṣma)* and undifferentiated *(avyakta)* form. But in the state of creation *(sṛṣṭi)*, the same principle, the inconscient nature *(prakṛti)* comes to acquire the patent, the gross and the differentiated objects of variegated names and forms. But, irrespective of its state in dissolution or creation, *prakṛti* is co-eternal with Brahman: it is always a mode *(prakāra)* of Brahman; it is 'of a tissue with Him', a phrase that at once suggests that the *apṛthak-siddhi* relation between Brahman and matter is not merely unique but organic. Hence Rāmānuja thinks that this *apṛthak-siddhi* relation between Brahman and *prakṛti* is a substantive-attributive relation: In this relation Brahman is the substance *(prakārin)*, the controller *(niyantṛ)*, the support *(ādhāra)*, the whole *(aṁśin)* and the principal *(śeṣin)*, even as *prakṛti*, or *acit*, is the mode *(prakāra)*, the controlled *(niyāmya)*, the supported *(dhārya, ādheya)*, the part *(aṁśa)* and the accessory *(śeṣa)*. We will see later that this same categorization of relation bears upon Rāmānuja's philosophy of religion, where the *apṛthak-siddhi* relation between Brahman and the self is given a paramount importance. This will be discussed in my next chapter.

Brahman and World Related as Cause and Effect

The entire universe, according to Rāmānuja, has sprung into being from Brahman, is sustained by it and will ultimately return to it. Therefore Brahman is the source of the universe in its evolution and involution alike. Since Brahman is the source that is the be-all and end-all of the universe, Rāmānuja combines in it the material, the operative and the accessory causes of the universe. Since creation is a real change *(pariṇāma)*, all the rudiments, that are to differentiate within Brahman, reside within Brahman in the shape of its power. This goes to suggest that Brahman is not a static but essentially a dynamic reality; within this dynamism, we ought to trace the roots of creation. Therefore Rāmānuja thinks that Brahman is the immanent ground of all existence, the source of all life and the home of all eternal values. It is the first and final cause; the root and the fruit, the whole and sole explanation of the world. Its pervasiveness in its creation is total, in the sense that it is above all in all and through all, all things are out of it, in it, and unto it. What is the nature of this causality that Rāmānuja advocates in respect of the world as its effect?

To Rāmānuja, the universal causality of Brahman in respect of the world is a fact borne out by both scriptures and reason. He quotes passages after passages to establish that Brahman stands in a universal causal relation to the world. He also has a detailed discussion on the nature of causality itself. As a *satkārya-vādin,* he argues for the prior existence of the effect in the cause. The causal operation is only for making patent what existed merely latently. Under the impact of this theory of *satkārya*, Rāmānuja maintains that Brahman is both the operative as well as the material cause. Despite the several, often mutually exclusive, currents in the *upaniṣads,* Rāmānuja identifies *satkārya-vāda* as the basic view of the *upaniṣads*. They describe the emanation of the world from Brahman on the analogy of the sparks which proceed from fire, or the web woven by the spider out of its own substance. Rāmānuja is convinced that both the analogy and the implicit theory of causality are consonant with the promissory declaration and the illustrative instances. The promissory declaration refers to what the scriptures assure as that there is a 'knowledge of the one that leads us to the knowledge of all *(ekavijñāne-sarva-vijñānam)*.'[13] The illustrative instances are those which bear upon our day to day knowledge of the effect resultant upon our knowledge of the cause.[14] We know it from our experience that oil is produced from oil-seeds and not from sand; oil is potentially existent in the oil-seeds. The causal operation of pressing the oil-seeds only brings the effect in actuality. To be sure, Rāmānuja admits that there are scriptural passages that declare *prakṛti* to be the eternal and the material cause of the world. But Rāmānuja points out that *prakṛti* in such passages denotes none other than Brahman itself, in its causal phase though, when names and forms are not yet distinguished. This interpretation is consistent here because there is no other principle independent of Brahman.[15] Besides, the scriptures directly and explicitly state that Brahman alone is the material as well as the operative cause of the world: 'Brahman was the wood, Brahman the tree, from which they shaped heaven and earth.'[16]

There are certain problems in making Brahman both the efficient and the material cause of the world, and also in making Brahman the formal and the material cause of the world. In the first case, it would appear that there should be a distinction between agency and that on which the efforts of agency are exerted. In the second case, it would appear that in making Brahman the formal and the material cause of the world, we would not be able to account for the imperfections inherent in the world. In both the cases, the question that we have to confront is: How can the perfect Brahman be the cause of an imperfect world? How can the perfect one differentiate itself into finite things? This problem is more than a philosophical riddle to Rāmānuja; he reads in it a profound sense of mystery, as he accepts it to be a fact. But Rāmānuja has not allowed this sense of mystery overpower his philosophical responsibility of explicating it. It is here that he does draw from the Sāṁkhya theory of causality. The general rule within *sat-kārya-vāda* is that an effect is pre-existent or co-existent in its cause. Therefore the world as an effect ought to have a certain homogeneity with Brahman its cause. The world then cannot be radically different from Brahman, in the sense of having a total independence from Brahman. Yet, the kind of homogeneity that Rāmānuja has in his mind is not the complete sameness of all attributes in the cause and effect. Indeed, if it were the complete sameness between the two, then, it would not only amount to identity, but also within identity there would be no scope for causal relation itself. Hence Rāmānuja points out that between cause and effect, there is some similarity as well as some dissimilarity; this indeed is the case with regard to Brahman and the world.

It may however be objected that Brahman cannot be the material cause of the world because, while the essential distinguishing characteristics of a causal substance would persist in its effect also, the world has the opposite of Brahman's essential nature. Brahman's nature is antagonistic to all evil, whereas the world, the effected Brahman, is seen to be with evil and all imperfections. Rāmānuja replies to the objection that homogeneity of cause and effect, in *sat-kārya-vāda,* does not require that all the attributes of the cause should pass over in its entirety into the effect also. It is quite conceivable that cause may give rise to an effect that may have a considerably different nature from the cause. Rāmānuja's example, of sentient worms being produced from the non-sentient honey, may well be off the mark, but his philosophical perception, that all the attributes of the cause need not pass into the effect, is quite sound. Otherwise there would be only identity, and not causal perception at all. Thus it is possible to conceive that a world differing in character from Brahman may originate from the latter.[17]

Rāmānuja is quick to point out that, since the world as the effect of Brahman differs in nature from Brahman, their difference in nature does not mean their total separateness. As cause and effect, Brahman and the world do possess some elements of similarity as well. It is these elements of similarity that make for the world's 'oneness' with Brahman. In what sense however can we say that the world is one with Brahman? Aware of this difficulty, Rāmānuja carefully analyses the causal relationship. He examines the causal theories propounded by various schools of thoughts; he points out the inadequacies of these theories, not only the non-Vedāntic but also the Advaitic; he then places before us his own theory of what may be termed as *brahma-pariṇāma-vāda*, as both distinct from, and, as a variation of, the Sāṁkhya's *prakṛti-pariṇāma-vāda*. Both, no doubt, are forms of *sat-kārya-vāda*, but its alteration in the hands of Rāmānuja is necessitated by a Vedāntic hermeneutics. According to this theory, Rāmānuja upholds the view that cause and effect are one and the same substance, but in two different states. The causal substance passes on from the causal state to the effect states. The two states have identity of substance but also the differentiated states, in which they may have different attributes.

Thus, for example, the jar, which is an effect, has the causal substance clay; and yet the jar has assumed another configuration and name in its effect state. It is one in substance with clay, and yet different from its causal substance, insofar as it has attributes, which are different from those of clay in its causal state. The effect is one with the cause, in the sense that it is potentially contained in the causal substance as a state, which this substance is capable of assuming.[18] In this way the effect is consubstantial with the causal substance and, yet, has a different nature of its own, in virtue of the new properties that it has acquired in its effect state. Applying these perceptions of *sat-kārya-vāda*, Rāmānuja argues that Brahman and the world are related as cause and effect. The world is consubstantial with Brahman, insofar as the world is none other than the causal Brahman, that potentially contains the world. But once the world has manifested itself as the effect world, it is none other than the effect Brahman with all its variegated actualities. They are one in substance, yet many in nature. Thus the world is one with Brahman, yet also different from Brahman.

Once the problem of substance and nature in causality is solved, Rāmānuja addresses himself to the problem of the one and the same Brahman being the efficient and the material cause of the world. This he does by way of introducing into the idea of cause the concept of growth borrowed from the organic world. He does it mainly to avoid the idea of the external agency, which we normally find in the case of causal operation. Thus, for example, in the case of a jar that is produced out of clay, we have the external agency of the potter. How about the causal operation of Brahman in respect of the world? With a clear vision of benefitting from his organismic conception of Brahman's causality in regard to the world, he writes,

> The case of the cause and effect is thus analogous to that of the child and youth. The word 'effect' denotes nothing else but the causal substance which has passed over into a different condition.[19]

Rāmānuja thus argues that in this way Brahman, as the cause , must be thought to be one in substance with the world. He understands by this that Brahman holds the world within itself in a potential form, and that creation is only the passing over of Brahman from one state of existence into another state of existence; in the former state of existence, the world exists potentially and in the latter state of existence the world exists actually. Brahman is regarded as existing in the periodically alternating states. Those states are referred to as the causal state *(kāraṇāvasthā)* and effect state *(kāryāvasthā)*. Whereas Brahman in the first state is the causal substance of the world, in the second state it is the actual manifestation of the world. So the creation *(sṛṣṭi)* of the world would only mean the actualisation of what is potential. What exists as a real possibility in the causal state turns out to be an actuality in the effect state, - a process that Rāmānuja attempts to understand in an organismic way.

It is of interest to note that Rāmānuja associates the evolution of the world of matter with that of the conscient world of selves. Both are the modes of Brahman when we say that Brahman exists in two states, causal and effect; it also means that the world of matter and selves too admit two different states. As for the self is concerned, when its *karma* requires a temporary but total cessation of evolution, its intelligence gets contracted. Corresponding to the contraction of intelligence of the selves, matter too gets into a dormant state; it becomes unevolved, as its evolution is for the fructification of the *karma* of the selves. Now, the two exists in Brahman, as its potentiality in a dormant state. Rāmānuja reads this quiescent state in the celebrated *upaniṣadic* statement, 'Being alone was there in the beginning, one without a second' *(sadeva-saumya-idam-agra-āsīt-ekamevādvitiyam)*.[20] Creation is the evolved state wherein the self's intelligence becomes expanded and, accordingly, for the fructification of its *karma* there is also the evolution of the matter.

What is of importance to Rāmānuja is that both evolution and involution thus signify the two states of the same substance of Brahman who, at all time, is qualified by matter and souls. The ultimate reality of Brahman is a triune unity: in one state it is differentiated into names and forms, whereas in another state it is still undifferentiated. Nonetheless, in both the states, Brahman's unity is not rejected, although it is sometimes in a homogeneous state and other times in a heterogeneous state. Both these states are equally real, none is false. Rāmānuja argues that, when the *upaniṣads* declare 'non-being' to be the source of all existence,[21] 'non-being', is not to be equated with 'non-existing'; it is rather to be understood as latent, or the causal, state of Brahman, as is expressly clarified by the *Bṛhadāraṇyaka Upaniṣad:* 'verily, at that time the world was undifferentiated. It becomes differentiated just by name and form.'[22]

Needless to say, the type of causality, that Rāmānuja subscribes to, has had its impact on his understanding of the relation between Brahman and *acit-prapañca*. We may, for a while, briefly compare it with Śaṁkara's understanding of causation. Transcendentally speaking, causation has no value in Śaṁkara's philosophy, which is substantially a philosophy of identity. And yet, for phenomenal purposes, Śaṁkara cannot but accept the value of the world. This would force him to work out a synthesis of causation with identity. I am afraid, his synthesis could not emerge, since he simultaneously accepts and denies causation. He then rightly has recourse to *vivarta-vāda,* or the theory of the illusoriness of the world. The result is the denial of the world, in the final analysis. For *vivarta-vāda* first posits a world through the law of causation, only to deny it at a later stage through indicating the illusoriness of the position, and thus thereby assert the reality of identity.[23] The doctrine of *vivarta-vāda* may be in conformity with the logic of identity and transcendental oneness of Brahman. But it cannot reconcile causation with identity; this is so because causation is a relational concept, whereas identity denies all relation. And yet, causation is the necessity of thought, whereas identity hopes to transcend thought itself. Therefore, Śaṁkara is unable to reconcile the claims of identity and causation, to some extent even at the empirical level and, to a greater extent, at the transcendental level. Hence his solution has been the retaining of identity at the cost of the world. Along with this, goes the reality of the immanent existence, dear to the Vedāntic spirit.

Rāmānuja, aware of the difficulties in Śaṁkara's understanding of causality, refuse to surrender the law of causation to the logic of identity. He is here much closer to Sāṁkhya than any other Vedāntin. He believes in the dynamic view of causation, though we would grant that this dynamism is at once spiritual and material, and not merely material in the Sāṁkhya way. As distinct from the static identity, Rāmānuja establishes a dynamic unity, in which identity and difference are reconciled. Therefore he is in a much happier situation of synthesising identity with causation. Causal action to him is to make explicit what is implicit in identity. While effect is latent in the cause, cause too persists in the effect. Causation therefore is nothing but a manifestation, a manifestation from the latent to patent stage and, again, from the patent to the latent stage. On a cosmic level, it is not the sort of transformation which obtains between milk that becomes curd; for here there is no possibility of re-transformation. To Rāmānuja, the transformation that is involved at the cosmic level is the one, in which the world-effect appears out of its cause, Brahman; and, again, it disappears back into its cause, Brahman. Therefore in either case, it is the transformation of Brahman from one state to the other. In the first case, the manifestation of the world is the effect-state of Brahman; in the second case, the involution of the world is the causal-state of the same Brahman. It is the one substance of Brahman that passes through the two states. It is the being that can be the cause of becoming. The one alone can become the many. It is the identity that can bring about difference, and yet be synthesized, for Rāmānuja. In the organismic scheme of Rāmānuja's metaphysics, all things are eternal and form a part, or mode of Brahman; Brahman is above all and abides in all. This position fully does justice to the immanent existence of the cause into all its effect, namely of Brahman in the world.

Brahman and World Related as Soul and Body

Once we have rightly understood the nature of Brahman's causality in respect of the world, it should not be difficult for us to understand why Rāmānuja considers that the world is the body and the attribute of Brahman. Brahman himself is conceived as the soul and the substance of the world. Let us have a closer look at Rāmānuja's thinking here.

There is a sense in which it could be said that Rāmānuja subscribes to *brahma-pariṇāma-vāda,* that is not valid to the Advaitin. Then, what becomes of Brahman, if there is to be a change of Brahman? In order to indicate both the nature and implication of change in Brahman, he speaks of the *apṛthak-siddhi-bhāva* in terms of the body soul relation *(śarīra-śarīri-bhāva)* between the world and Brahman. To Rāmānuja, Brahman is the soul that represents its own perfect nature, and the body that part of the self same Brahman which is the world. ·Rejecting the common sense definitions of body in merely physicalistic sense, Rāmānuja thinks that body is,

> Any substance which a sentient soul is capable of completely controlling and supporting for its own purpose, and which stands to the soul in an entirely subordinate relation.... In this sense, then ... non-sentient being... constitutes the body of the supreme person, for they are completely controlled and supported by Him for His own ends, and are absolutely subordinate to Him.[24]

The idea of Brahman as the *śarīrin,* or the embodied soul, logically follows from his organismic ontology. Brahman is the *śārīrika* because he is the 'manifested soul'; the entire *prakṛti,* the principle of the world, is the manifestation of his power. The latter constitutes Brahman's body; as his body, it is subservient to him, supported by him; and in *pralaya*, it is reduced to the subtle condition by him. Hence, Brahman is the very ground *(ādhāra)* of the universe, while the latter is supported *(ādheya)* by him. Once again, the Vedāntic hermeneutician that he is, Rāmānuja traces back his ideas of Brahman serving as the indwelling soul of the world to the *Antaryāmī-brāhmaṇa* of the *Bṛhadāraṇyaka Upaniṣad*, a point that is further reinforced by the *Muṇḍaka* and the *Śvetāśvatara Upaniṣads.*[25]

Now, to return to the question, if the modification of Brahman in the world does not introduce any imperfection in his nature. Rāmānuja rules out the traces of any imperfection in Brahman in the context of his modification because, he believes, all changes occur in the body of Brahman, namely *prakṛti* and not its soul. Hence, any imperfection that may be said to be brought about in the process of change affect only the *acit-prapañca*. He writes,

> While the highest Self thus undergoes a change in the form of world comprising ... non-sentient beings, all imperfections ... and changes are restricted to the non-sentient things which constitute his part .... Their inner Ruler and Self, (He) is in no way touched by their imperfections and changes.[26]

Thus it may be stated that Brahman is in the world, but not as the world. The *acit-prapañca* has its form and functions in Brahman. Brahman's causality, in respect of the manifested world, is so complete that He is the first and the final cause of all things therein; He is the root of life as well as its fruit. He is the immanent ground, and inner sustaining power, of the *acit-prapañca*. This concept of Brahman as the inner soul of the world shows that the finite is not only rooted in, but is also controlled by, the infinite: the finite has its source and sustenance in the infinite, but the infinite is not exhausted by the finite. The chief value of this concept lies in its emphasis on the divine sovereignty without in any way endangering, or minimising, the reality and existence of the finite world. Yet another form, that Rāmānuja chooses to explicate the *apṛthak-siddhi-bhāva*, is this that Brahman is the substance whereas the world is the attribute of the former.

While the explanation of the relation between Brahman and the world is given in terms of the body-soul relation, in virtue of his organismic metaphysics, the same relation is also explicated by Rāmānuja in terms of substance and attribute, in virtue of his realistic epistemology. Both by empirical reasoning and by an appeal to the scriptures, Rāmānuja contends against the concept of a Brahman being regarded as pure Being; he rather contends for a Brahman who is regarded as a unity which includes differences within itself. This conception of a differentiated Brahman prepares the ground for his view that Brahman and the world are related as substance and attribute. He is of the view that a substantive-attributive relation holds good not only in the case of objects and their generic qualities, but also in the case of the distinct objects: in the latter case, one object may be considered as the attribute of the other. For example, in the notion of 'staff-bearer', the 'staff' is a separable predicate to its 'bearer'. It is separable because it can exist by itself apart from its bearer. Again, in the notion of 'rational man', rationality is an inseparable predication of man. It is inseparable because it makes for the inner differentiation within man. Rāmānuja would argue that both types of attributes hold the same relationship with a substance, namely the substantive-attributive relation.

Once it is granted that Brahman is a substance, qualified by attributes, and that attributes need not necessarily be only generic (e.g. *satyam, jñānam* etc.), Rāmānuja sees no difficulty in treating the world as an attribute, or a mode, of Brahman. To be sure, like the staff in our above example the world too is, in a sense, substantive, and not merely attributive. The world with all its plurality may be accepted as real, and as having a substance of its own; and yet, that reality and the substantiality can also be attributive in relation to Brahman insofar as it exixts in and for Brahman; again, insofar as it accounts for the differentiated Brahman. Because it is an inner differentiation, the predication of the world does not endanger the unity of Brahman, its substance. Thus Rāmānuja argues for the difference of the world from Brahman and, at the same time, its complete dependence on Brahman. This distinction and yet dependence of *acit-prapañca* is given expression to epistemologically by his substantive-attributive relation. This is a new way of the application of *apṛthak-siddhi-bhāva* between Brahman and *acit*.

Rāmānuja also attempts to explicate the substantive-attributive relation in terms of his theory of causation. An effect is nothing other than an attribute, or a mode, of the causal substance. When we speak of the production of an effect from a cause, it only means that a substance, characterized by a certain attribute, or state, or mode, of existence, assumes another attribute, or state or mode of existence. The latter must therefore be presumed to have existed in the former always potentially. *Acit* then exists always in Brahman; it is Brahman's eternal attribute, or mode. It becomes *acit-prapañca*; this too continues to be the attribute, or mode, of Brahman. Thus the causal Brahman becomes the effect Brahman in virtue of the causal operation. A perceptive philosopher will see, Rāmānuja argues, how it is the same soul-body relationship that has now become the substance-attribute relationship. Since body is completely dependent on the soul, it ceases to exist when separated from the soul. Even so an attribute, or mode, is thought to be so completely dependent on its substance that, when separated from the latter, it ceases to exist. Hence, the attribute, or mode, cannot but be perennially supported by the substance, to which it belongs. In this way, *acit-prapañca* is nothing but a mode, an attribute, of Brahman. What is more, in virtue of this ontological dependence, all knowledge of the world too is dependent on the knowledge of its substance Brahman.

Just as he had obviated the problem of the imperfection of the body imputing on the soul, here too, Rāmānuja asserts that the imperfection of the mode does not affect its substance; the imperfection of the effected world does not taint the immaculate nature of Brahman. He writes,

> Whenever we cognise the relation of distinguishing attribute and the thing distinguished thereby, the two clearly present themselves to our mind as absolutely different.[27]

Needless to say, Rāmānuja relies on his realistic epistemology here more than he does anywhere else. He thinks that difference in characteristics of the mode from those of the substance therefore need not alarm us; such difference is quite the usual characteristic of the modes. What makes something a mode is not the sameness of character with the substance to which it belongs, but complete dependence. In virtue of this complete dependence, it is a mode, but in virtue of its distinction, it is all that it is. Its imperfections are its own, and they do not reflect on its substance. Hence, Rāmānuja concludes that the whole world is,

> predicative to, or mode of, *parama-puruṣa;* hence *parama-puruṣa* alone exists adjectivated by everything else. All terms are thus connotations of Him by the rule of *samānādhikaraṇya*, or the rule which expresses the inseparable relation existing between substance and attribute, or the invariable co-existence of subject and predicate.[28]

In such a relation, the imperfections of the predicates are said to be not sullying the nature of *parama-puruṣa*.

A question that we need to raise here pertains to the capacity of *acit* to reflect Brahman. The question is rather unpleasant to scholars of Rāmānuja Vedānta. Hence I am not surprised that most scholars have conveniently ignored it. Though there could be many philosophical problems associated with Rāmānuja's thinking here, I should at least venture to state it here, if not really solve it. *Acit* is a reality *(tattva)* that is fundamentally inconscient *(jaḍa)*. When *acit* evolves into the world of variegatedness, does it adequately reflect Brahman who is a conscient reality? Rāmānuja answers the question in the affirmative. He thinks that, though matter is *jaḍa*, it has its 'intelligency', as it were, because it is a mode, an attribute of Brahman. The variegated world is causal Brahman, that has become the effect Brahman, who is perennially the conscious reality. Just as the consciousness of an intelligent being is not perceived, when it is in the state of deep sleep, swoon, the 'intelligent' nature of *prakṛti* and its products too is not observed, although it really exists, however minimal it may be in different circumstances. What finally accounts for the difference between Brahman and *acit* is not the radical and the qualitative distinction; it is rather the difference of manifestation and non-manifestation of intelligence; the distinction of intelligent and non-intelligent beings depends on this manifestation or otherwise. This view ultimately leads to the conclusion that Brahman is substance and *prakṛti* is its attribute. However persuasive this thinking, I am afraid, it takes away the differentiation between the *tattva-trayas* admitted in Rāmānuja Vedānta. What is more, we would be at a greater loss to account for the difference between *cit* and *acit* too.

It is of some interest to note that *acit*, which is a mode of Brahman, admitting an internal difference, is itself said to be a triad of some kind. Through this triadic unity, *acit* or *prakṛti*, is said to reflect Brahman himself. Therefore, just as Brahman is a triadic unity, or a unity in 'trinity', *prakṛti* too is conceived to be a triadic unity of *sattva, rajas* and *tamas*. These threefold characteristics are further said to give rise in the process of world-creation to the elements of fire, water and earth. The world-play, or the variegatedness, is attributed to the various permutations of these elements. Surprisingly, Rāmānuja's explication of the creation of the world in terms of triplication *(trivṛtkaraṇa)* strikes a rather odd note in the Indian philosophical tradition, though it is not inconsistent with the earliest Vedic tradition. For what is much more universally accepted in Indian cosmology is the 'creation' of the world in terms of quintuplication *(pañcīkaraṇa),* to rightly name the world *'prapañca'*. Yet, if Rāmānuja digresses a bit here, it appears to me, he is impelled to seek a parallelism between the nature of Brahman and the nature of his mode. However inconscient this mode *acit* be, it too should reflect the threefold characters of *sattva, rajas* and *tamas*. These characters concretize in the gross elements of fire, water and earth, which account for the world's variegated colours and contours.

Thus, while placing before us the *apṛthak-siddhi* relation between Brahman and *acit-prapañca,* Rāmānuja first of all asserts the reality of the world, its continued existence and finally its involution in Brahman and, at the same time, the sovereignty of Brahman. But, in discussing the triplication of the *acit-prapañca,* he is guided by the nature of Brahman whose mode it is. Hence the cosmic world is composed of three elements *(trivṛtkaraṇa),* that is earth, water and fire. Impelled by the omnipotent will of Brahman, the undifferentiated subtle matter *(prakṛti)* gradually becomes manifold into three kinds of elements. But in this process the highest Brahman continues to be the author of the evolution of the world of names and forms. The view is not merely Vedic. The thread of the Vedic speculations percolate into the *upaniṣads* as well. Rāmānuja is aware of the text that distinctly bears upon the procession of the elements from *prakṛti*, residing in Brahman, and also of the indwelling of the same Brahman within the world of elements:

> That Being (i.e., that which has produced fire, water and earth) thought, let me now enter those three beings (fire, water and earth) with this living self *(jīvātma)* and let me then reveal (develop) names and forms.[29]

One of the important implications of *trivṛtkaraṇa,* that has created problems for Rāmānuja's theory of error *(khyātivāda),* is the thesis that everything is in everything. This thesis in part stems from his organismic metaphysics that within the heart of supreme person we are to locate everything that is, material, mental and spiritual. Those, accustomed to think of their distinction in radical terms, find it difficult to grasp why materiality and immateriality interpenetrate each other. Hence they find it difficult to understand the qualification of Brahman by *cit* and *acit,* even as they find it difficult to see that *acit* includes within itself an element of *cit,* and is finally ruled by Brahman from within. It is the same spirit of organismic theory that pervades his discussion of the elements, bringing about the world of triplication.

Against this backdrop, we should understand what Rāmānuja says about the burning fire, that includes within itself both water and earth, or about the sweating body that includes fire and water, and so on. Thus he would identify the different colours of the burning fire with the different elements that are in combination with fire itself. This means that forms of fire are themselves due to triplication of the three elements. For example, 'the red colour sensation in the burning fire comes from primal elementary fire, the white colour from water, the black colour from earth'; and finally, the indeterminate colour is due to the combination of the three beings.

The same principle holds good in the case of all things, everything being composed or compounded of all the three primary elements, with due regard to the dominant element therein and the proportion of the combination of the elements concerned. Hence in all valid and invalid perceptions we do apprehend all three elements, however minimal they be. The triplication of elements, that is first spoken of in respect of the evolution of names and forms for the explanation of the external world, is further extended by Rāmānuja to the body of man as well. The body is said to consist of these three elements, and it is obvious from the effects thereof: the sweat, the digestion and the smell. Thus to Rāmānuja, the mention of any one element implies the other two elements too. Fire is with water and earth, water is combined with fire and earth, even as earth is associated with fire and water, by its very nature.

Thus the threefold nature of Brahman is reflected in the threefold nature of *prakṛti,* or *cit,* which is the mode of Brahman. *Prakṛti,* or *cit,* too reflects that threefold nature of Brahman in the elements of fire, water and earth. The elements in return manifest the qualities of *sattva, rajas,* and *tamas* in all the objects, constituted by the elements of *prakṛti*. The whole creation then exhibits, as it were, the nature of Brahman itself; in this sense, the creation now is the body, an extension of the supreme reality. Rāmānuja is close to the etymological significance of not only 'Brahman' ('that which has burst forth', 'extended'), but also of '*jagat*' ('that which has manifested'). We should note here that it is not only *prakṛti* that has three *guṇas* of *sattva, rajas,* and *tamas;* but that Brahman too, in a sense, may be said to have been endowed with them. In virtue of *rajas*, he is Brahmā, the creator; in virtue of *sattva,* he is Viṣṇu, the preserver; and in virtue of *tamas,* he is Rudra, the destroyer. We cannot but appreciate the successful way in which Rāmānuja integrates the philosophy of the *Purāṇas* with his Vedānta.

This way of looking at Brahman's causality in respect of the world, and of conceiving the *apṛthak-siddhi* relation between Brahman and *acit-prapañca*, highlights an important aspect of Rāmānuja's philosophy. In virtue of his organismic unity of Brahman, it is not the opposition between matter and spirit that is important to Rāmānuja. It is rather their marvellous unity and complementarity that is close to the heart of Rāmānuja's philosophy. Therefore, due to the threefold nature of Brahman, and thereafter, of *prakṛti*, there is always a harmony between Brahman and *prakṛti*. This is made possible by the fact of the inseparable relation between the two.

Rāmānuja therefore is much closer to the scriptures, when he thinks that the world is a triad of name, form and work, than any other Vedāntin, who narrowly restricts it to name and form *(nāma-rūpa)* alone; he shows us that in order to read substancelessness in the world,[30] we need not deny the world; rather we need to show its complete dependence on Brahman. To Rāmānuja *acit-prapañca* is the body of Brahman and, as such, it proclaims the manifested glory of Brahman in virtue of the *apṛthak-siddhi* relation obtained between the two.

References

1. *Śrībhāṣya,* Thibaut's Introduction, pp. xxiv-v.
2. Rāmānuja is not the only Vedāntin to reject *māyā-vāda* of Advaita. It has evoked strong protests from all other schools of Vedānta: Madhva, Nimbārka, Vallabha, Jñānadeva and, in modern times, Aurobindo. All these thinkers have followed considerably the similar line of criticism against Advaita as is followed by Rāmānuja.
3. *Śvetāśvatara Upaniṣad,* IV:9.
4. *Kaṭha Upaniṣad,* 1, 3.12.
5. *Bṛhadāraṇyaka Upaniṣad,* II.1.20.
6. *Ibid*, 1.4.5.
7. *Bṛhadāraṇyaka Upaniṣad,* 1.4.7; *Chāndogya Upaniṣad*, VI.2.
8. *Bṛhadāraṇyaka Upaniṣad,* 1.4.7.
9. *Bṛhadāraṇyaka Upaniṣad,* 1.4.16; II.1; V.II.5, III.7, III.9, IV.4.13' *Chāndogya Upaniṣad,* V.18.1.2; *Taittirīya Upaniṣad,* II.6; *Kauśitaki Upaniṣad,* 4; *Īśa Upaniṣad,* 1.6; *Kaṭha Upaniṣ ad,* V.9.13; *Muṇḍaka Upaniṣad,* II.1.4.9; *Śvetāśvatara Upaniṣ ad,* 1.16; VI.11, VI.34.
10. *Bṛhadāraṇyaka Upaniṣad*, 3.7.
11. *The Gītā,*VII.6; IX.7, 8, 10, 17; X. 39; XIV.3.
12. *Gītā* IX.7, 9. *Śvetāśvatara Upaniṣad,* III.2, IV.1, V.3.
13. *Chāndogya Upaniṣad,* VI, 1.3.
14. *Chāndogya Upaniṣad* VI, 1.4; see also *Śrībhāṣya*, 1.4.23.
15. *Śrībhāṣya,* 1.4.23.
16. *Rigveda* X: 30ff; *Śrībhāṣya,* 1.4.25.
17. *Ibid,* II.1.4.
18. *Ibid,* II.1.15.
19. *Śrībhāṣya,* II.1.16.
20. *Chāndogya Upaniṣad* , 4: 2,1.
21. *Taittirīya Upaniṣad,* II.7.
22. *Bṛhadāraṇyaka Upaniṣad*, 1: 4.7.

23. *Saṁksepa-śāriraka of Sarvajñātma Muni, Benaras Edition: Vivartavādasya hi pūrva bhūmih vedāntavāde pariṇāmavādaḥ* \ *Vyavasthitesmin pariṇāmavāde svayaṁ samayati vivartavādaḥ* \\, p. 40.
24. *Śrībhāṣya,* II.1.9.
25. *Muṇḍaka Upaniṣad,* II. 1,4,9; *Śvetāśvatara Upaniṣad,* VI. 11.
26. *Śrībhāṣya,* 1.4.27.
27. *Gītābhāṣya,* VII.7.
28. *Śrībhāṣya,* I. 1.1.1.
29. *Chāndogya Upaniṣad,* 6.3.2.
30. *Ibid,* 11.6.

5

Apṛthak-Siddhattva between Brahman and *Cit-prapañca*

This chapter will highlight the application of *apṛthak-siddhattva* between Brahman and *ātman* in Rāmānuja's metaphysics. Like *acit, cit* too is a mode of Brahman, and it is inseparably related with Brahman. This relation of inseparability which holds between Brahman and *cit,* or *ātman,* is, to Rāmānuja, more important than the same relation between Brahman and *acit-prapañca,* or *jagat*. It is because of the fact that he was intensely concerned with safeguarding the autonomy of the individual selves that are co-eval with Brahman, be it in bondage or in liberation. Moreover, it is here that Rāmānuja proves himself to be not merely an eminent metaphysician but also a pre-eminent Vedāntic philosopher of religion. After discussing the nature of this inseparable relation, explicated in terms of many models, between *ātman* and Brahman, I will also discuss how the finite self, or *ātman,* is absolutely dependent on Brahman's will. Is there a conflict then between the autonomy and the heteronomy of dependence of the *cit* on Brahman? If there be some sort of a conflict between the two, how does Rāmānuja overcome it? Finally, I will address myself to the question of this relation both in bondage and release. It would seem that at least in release this *apṛthak-siddhattva* between Brahman and *cit* should break down. This however is not the case in Rāmānuja's metaphysics. For release is not a mere release from the bondage; it is positively a release into the realization of this inseparability with Brahman.

Having recourse to my comparative method, I would like to contrast the views of Rāmānuja with those of Advaita on the relation between Brahman and *ātman*. This relation is succinctly expressed by the Advaitin in his celebrated thesis that *jīva* is not other than Brahman *(jīvo-brahmaiva nā paraḥ)*. Needless to say, this negation of a separate and independent status to the self is consistent with the pure non-dualistic philosophy. Accordingly, to Advaita Vedānta, Brahman alone is the supreme and the sole reality; all the finite selves are nothing but the appearances of Brahman. The infinite appears as finite self (or selves) through the adjunct of *māyā,* or *avidyā*. To be fair to Advaitin, Advaitin makes a distinction between the relation that obtains between individual self and Brahman on the one hand, and the relations that obtains between the world and Brahman on the other. Whereas the world *(jagat)* of experience is straightaway negated as an 'illusion', though not devoid of the substratum of Brahman, the individual self is 'negated' by way of asserting the identity of the self with Brahman; it is said to be no other *(na-paraḥ)* than Brahman. Hence, in the latter case, there is no question of any relation between the two, because in asserting their identity, there really is no duality at all. Whatever sense of 'twoness' that is entertained here is once again due to the adjunct of nescience *(avidyā), which* is the subjectivated aspect of *māyā* itself.

In order to support their contention, the Advaitin's take the help of the illustrious scriptural texts *(mahāvākya)*, in particular, of such identity statements as 'That thou art' *(tat-tvaṁ-asi)*. They interpret that *tat* refers to the innermost core, or essence, of Brahman that is the substratum of the world process. It may be viewed as the essence of the objective world. Likewise, *tvaṁ* refers to the innermost core, or essence, of the same Brahman that sustains the world of the conscient and individual selves. It may be viewed as the essence of the subjective world. Advaitin asserts that the essence of the objective and subjective world is the one, non-dual, immutable Brahman. Other *mahā-vākyas* too, such as *sarvaṁ-khalu-idaṁ-brahman, ekamevādvitīyaṁ* etc. convey the same identity between the essence of macrocosm and microcosm, the objective and the subjective world.

This pure non-dualistic understanding of reality is not acceptable to Rāmānuja. He rather subscribes to the thesis that the ultimate reality, or Brahman, is an internally differentiated being *(svagata-bheda)*, that admits within itself the realities of the conscient selves *(cit)* and the inconscient matter *(acit)* as the modes *(prakāra)* of Brahman. Therefore, as a Vedāntin he too interprets *mahā-vākya, tat-tvaṁ-asi*, in a way consistent with his own perception of Brahman as the internally differentiated ultimate, or the Being qualified *(viśiṣṭasya, guṇī)* by *cit* and *acit*. Before he presents us with his own interpretation, Rāmānuja explains that the *mahā-vākyas* are not meant to convey the idea of the absolute unity of a non-differentiated substance; on the contrary, they denote a Brahman distinguished by difference. Therefore, Brahman is by its very nature a relational entity, and it can be grasped only by a philosophical method that bears upon relatedness. Thus the term, 'that' in the *mahā-vākya* concerned, refers to Brahman in his utter transcendence, therefore in its unmanifest form *(avyakta)*; nevertheless, it is the unmanifest that is intrinsically qualified. The word 'thou', in virtue of its standing in co-ordination *(samānādhikaranya)* to 'that', conveys the idea of the Brahman in his total immanence, the manifest form *(vyakta)* that has for its body the individual selves.[1] What must not be overlooked here is that Brahman both in manifest and unmanifest forms is qualified reality. He writes,

> Indeed, both the terms *that* and *thou,* when put in a predication of identity *(samānādhikaraṇya)* signify Brahman alone. The term *that* refers to Brahman, who is the cause of the universe, the abode of all auspicious qualities; the flawless and the changeless one; whereas the term *thou* signifies that same Brahman; who, because he is the inner controller of finite selves, has these selves, along with their bodies, as His modes.[2]

In the course of explaining the *sadvidyā*, at the beginning of the *Vedārtha-saṁgraha,* Rāmānuja states his distinctive doctrine of the relation between Brahman and the individual self as under:

> The finite self *(jīvātma)* has Brahman as the self, for it is His mode *(prakāra),* since it is the body *(śarīra)* of Brahman.[3]

He derives support for his thesis from *śṛti* and *smṛti* before he has recourse to *tarka.*[4] The most celebrated scriptural text that Rāmānuja is never tired of quoting is the *Antaryāmī-brāhmaṇa* of the *Bṛhadāraṇyaka Upaniṣad* (III.7.22):

> He who dwells in the self and within the self, whom the self does not know, of whom the self is the body, within, He is thyself, the Ruler within, the immortal.

Likewise, the *smṛti* that he relies heavily on is the *Gītā* that clearly teaches the reality of individual self and its eternal distinction from Brahman. Rāmānuja firmly holds on to the declaration of the *Gītā* that 'An eternal part of myself (Brahman) becomes the individual self in the world of life.'[5] He now employs reason *(tarka)* for the same objective of proving this essential inseparability of the self from Brahman. In virtue of the inseparability of the self with Brahman, Rāmānuja contends that the real nature of the individual self cannot be known apart from that of God; since the two are inseparably and indissolubly related to each other, self cannot be epistemologically apprehended without apprehending the ultimate ground of its existence, viz. Brahman. Therefore the individual self is a part of Brahman.[6] This conclusion further finds support in the *Chāndogya Upaniṣad*[7] that says that the individual self, as a part, is apprehended only in the whole whose part it is.

When the individual self is said to be a part *(aṁśa)* of Brahman, it does not mean that it constitutes a part of the extension of Brahman. Such an understanding is clearly ruled out, since Brahman is partless. If we understand *apṛthak-siddhattva* in terms of part and whole *(aṁśa-aṁśi),* it must not be quantitatively imagined lest all the imperfections of the individual self should belong to Brahman too. The relation should rather be construed in its qualitative sense only. It then would mean that the self as a part of Brahman is a mode, or an attribute, *(prakāra)* of Brahman. Here too there is a need to add a caveat.

Though Rāmānuja regards the individual self as the attribute, or mode, of Brahman, it does not mean that the former has a mere adjectival existence only, with no individuality of its own. I had occasion in the previous chapter to show that, according to Rāmānuja, the substance-attribute relationship holds good not only in case of objects and their generic qualities, but also in the case of the different objects themselves. He does not see any contradiction in viewing one object in a substantive (or attributive, for that matter) relation with another object. In other words, objects, complete, whole and all by themselves, can enter into a substantive-attributive relation. Accordingly, the individual self may be an attribute of Brahman, and at the same time may have an individuality of its own. The individual self is conceived to be an attribute of Brahman only in the sense that it belongs to Brahman and is completely dependent on it. Thus *cit* has at once a substantive being of its own and also an adjectival existence within Brahman. The individual self in relation to Brahman is an attribute, even as Brahman in relation to self is its substance. It is this peculiar character, of completeness in being and yet of dependence in existence and activity, that Rāmānuja tries to capture in his notion of *apṛthak-siddhattva*.

The twofold characterization of the *cit*, as *prakāra* and *guṇa*, therefore the relation that obtains between Brahman and *cit*, are best captured by Rāmānuja in different models. But these models can all be subsumed under the 'body-soul relationship' *(śarīra-śarīri-bhāva)*, which may be considered as the key to his rich metaphysics: Brahman is the soul, and *cit* is the body of Brahman. The implication that Rāmānuja here draws are of interest to me:

> Because the finite selves are the body of the supreme self, they are modes of that self.[8]

Here, one of the implications is that the modality of *cit* is in virtue of its forming the body of Brahman. If we are to understand the body-soul relation between Brahman and *cit,* subsumed under any of the models, we first have to understand Rāmānuja's conception of body.

I am not prepared to buy the argument of some authors that Rāmānuja's belief, that finite selves constitute the body of the Supreme Self, is, for him, not the conclusion of a rational argument, but a fundamental fact vouched for by the scripture. He strongly believes that the authority of the scriptures must be corroborated by *tarka*. Accordingly, he aims at substantiating, by way of reasoning, that, because the finite selves constitute the body of Brahman, we can say that these selves are the modes of Brahman.[9] With this purport in his mind, he asks, what then is a body? I had briefly discussed it in the context of *apṛthak-siddhattva* between Brahman and *acit*. Since the application of *apṛthak-siddhattva* in relation to Brahman and *cit* is much more important, I shall build upon whatever is already stated in respect of 'body'. There are two definitions that Rāmānuja gives, the one in the *Śrībhāṣya* and the other in the *Vedārtha-saṁgraha*. Despite the charge of repetition, I will reproduce here the one given by the former, as it seems to be both exhaustive and incisive, and much needed for my present concerns:

> Any substance *(dravya)* that an intelligent being *(ātman)* is able completely to control *(niyantām)* and support *(dhārayitam)* for his own purposes, and the essential nature of which is entirely subservient *(śeṣatva)* to that intelligent self, - is his body.[10]

I am inclined to identify three important elements in the definition given above, that will have a direct bearing on the relationship between the self and the body in general, and on the extension of this relationship between Brahman and the individual self, in particular. Firstly the relation between body and soul is a relation between the support and what it supports; while the support may be said to exist all by itself, that which is supported is incapable of a separate existence *(pṛthak-siddhi-anarha)*. Secondly, the relation between the body and soul may also be said to be the relation between the controller and what is controlled. The support, in virtue of its independence in existence, becomes the controller, whereas what is supported is intrinsically controlled by the former. Thirdly, the relation between body and soul is the relation between the owner and what is owned. That what is owned is subservient to the owner, as is the case with some disposable property.

Everyone of these elements is used by Rāmānuja for both transforming, and thereafter for transferring, into a different realm the relation between Brahman and *cit,* when he applies the body-soul analogy to his metaphysics of relation. Whereas these models are spoken of with a cool philosophical sobriety in the *Śrībhāṣya* and, to some extent, in the *Vedārtha-saṁgraha*, they are spoken with a deep passion and pathos in the *Gītābhāṣya*. To illustrate the latter:

> In the heart of all beings, who constitute my body, I am seated as their Self *(ātma)*, for to be the 'Self' means that I am entirely their support *(ādhāra)*, controller *(niyantā)* and owner *(śeṣi)*.[11]

Again,

> Know that they all originated from me. They abide in Me, they are My body, but I am not in them, which is to say, I do not depend on them. In other cases, the self, though to be sure the one on whom its body depends, also derives some benefit from its body, but know that there is no benefit in them for Me. This means that my purpose is only and entirely sport ... I pervade the universe as its Inner Controller *(antaryāmī)*, in order to support it, and by virtue of being its Owner *(Śeṣi)*. I am the supporter of finite beings *(bhūta-bhṛt)*, but I derive no benefit from them.[12]

The application of the simile, of the dependence of the body on the soul, to Brahman and *cit* on the metaphysical plane, makes Rāmānuja open to serious objections. Indeed, such objections, in the context of causality though, were raised against Rāmānuja's similar understanding of the relation between Brahman and *acit* too; Rāmānuja had met them effectively. Likewise, he has now to face the charges against this relation in the context of the relation between Brahman and *cit*. In its most general form, the charge is that if Brahman were in such a soul-body relationship with the conscient selves, which are finite, he would be affected by the imperfection of the finite selves that constitute his cosmic body. Soul and body constitute one organism and, whatever defects that affect the body should redound to the extent to the sullying of the soul itself. If so whatever defect, to which the finite self is heir to, should tell upon the purity and perfection of Brahman too.

Rāmānuja faces this objection squarely. He answers that, first of all in the composite being of Brahman, each substance retains its distinctive nature. Therefore, in virtue of the retaining of its distinctive nature, it is possible to argue out that the imperfections of the body do not affect the self that ensouls it. What is more, the supreme Self is not subject to *karma*. It is *karma* that works as the cause of experiencing pain and other evils. Being free from *karma*, indeed being the Lord of *karma,* Brahman is not tainted by *karma;* nor does he experience its consequents of pain and pleasure. More positively, far from making for defects in God, the possession of bodies contributes towards the lordship *(īśītṛtva)* of Brahman. Each of these points can now be elucidated.

The combination of the conscient selves, in virtue of being the body of Brahman, in a sense considered as the 'material things', or the objects of enjoyment *(bhogya)*, with Brahman, does not confuse their differing nature. Brahman is in a sense the enjoyer-lord *(bhoktā)*, in virtue of his being the soul. Both Brahman and the finite self retain their own nature. Brahman retains at all stages his immaculate and pure spiritual nature. Even so, the finite self, too, retains its essential features of the spiritual-psycho-physical nature, when concorporated, and its spiritual nature when non-concorporated; it retains its consciousness and its capacity to experience enjoyment *(bhoktā),* even when it constitutes the organismic complex being. The complexity of union with Brahman thus in no way cancels the essential nature of *cit*. This, Rāmānuja argues, is analogous to a piece of cloth, woven with threads of three or more different colours, each thread however retaining its own colour. We should be careful here to admit the limitation of the analogy used. For, in the example cited, the different coloured threads can exist separately prior to their being woven together in the cloth. But in Rāmānuja's metaphysics, both matter and finite spirits constitute the body of Brahman both in the causal state, prior to their 'creation' and also in their state of 'relatedness', that is, in the stage of manifested world of objects and subjects. Hence their existence is always as modes of Brahman, causal or effected; they do not at any stage exist independent of Brahman.

Rāmānuja seems to be aware of the limitations of his analogy. For, having spoken of this soul-body relation between Brahman and *cit* he adds:

> In all states (the state of cause before creation and the state of effect afterward), Brahman has spiritual and material entities as His body.[13]

Again,

> Because the Supreme Self is their Inner Ruler and Self, He is not touched by their imperfection and mutation *(vikāra)*.[14]

This clearly indicates how keen Rāmānuja is to keep the pure nature of Brahman intact, even in union with the manifest world of subjects. By stating that, Brahman is the inner ruler of the finite self, he also asserts the presiding power of Brahman over *karma* too. This means positively that he dwells in a higher realm, or exists on a higher plane, that is not touched by the one subjected to the inexorable law of *karma*. On the contrary, he undergirds, pervades and contracts the transient realm afflicted with *karma* concretized in evil and imperfection. Going a step forward, he offers a much more positive aspect of this union in stating that the finite self (also the inconscient matter) serves to 'enhance' Brahman's lordship. This is an enhancement in the sense of the external glory manifested in his modes rather than what intrinsically adds to the inner nature of Brahman; the latter however lacks nothing and which always is perfect *(paripūrṇa)*. Fittingly is his philosophy called a *śārīraka darśana*. This however is only one of the meanings of the term *śārīraka* in his philosophy, as is evidenced from the following:

> Thus the entire group of intelligent and non-intelligent entities, which are different from Him, constitute his body, and he alone is the unconditioned self ensouling that body *(nirupādhikas-śarīra-ātma)*. For this very reason, competent authorities call this doctrine *(śāstra)*

concerning the supreme Brahman by the name 'śārīraka'; the doctrine of the 'embodied' Self.[15]

Rāmānuja's metaphysics is indeed this doctrine of the 'embodied' self, or *śārīrika-vidyā*: The ultimate reality is the Brahman embodied of *cit* and *acit*; and the relation that obtains between them is the relation of inseparability. This further conclusively brings out the need for viewing Rāmānuja's metaphysics through the specific perspective of relation. Such a relation Rāmānuja views through three important models: the relation of the supporter-supported *(ādhāra-ādheya)*, of the controller-controlled *(niyantṛ-niyāmya)* and the principal-accessory *(śeṣi-śeṣa)*. There are other secondary models too. I will however focus my attention on the threefold models here below:

Ādhāra literally means 'the support', 'the substratum', 'the container'; and *ādheya* means 'the supported', 'the inherent', 'the contained'. Brahman is *ādhāra,* occasionally and alternatively also termed, *āśraya*. In saying this Rāmānuja means that Brahman is the ultimate ground of all finite beings specially of the order of the conscient selves in virtue of his being the fullness of being, or Being itself; all beings have come forth out of Him. Rāmānuja uses the familiar Vedāntic analogy of the clay that remains the sole reality in all things that are made out of clay: 'As by one lump of clay there is made known all that is made of clay....'[16] By such *upaniṣadic* statements, Rāmānuja thinks that the concept of *ādhāra* adequately expresses the truth that the metaphysical highest, which is also at once the highest of the religious aspirations, is the ontic ground of finite being; the cause (both material and efficient) of its periodic transformation of states, on account of the requirements of the fructification of *karma*.

The transition from the metaphysical highest to the religious highest in Rāmānuja's thinking must not be overlooked. For all Vedāntins *tattva-vicāra* cannot be separated from *mokṣa-vicāra*. Rāmānuja is no exception here, although his concern takes on a distinctive theistic form. All finite beings are completely dependent *(ayatta)* on God for their essential nature *(svarūpa)*, continued existence in the phenomenal realm *(sthiti)*, and actual functioning, or activity *(pravṛtti)*.[17] In being *ādhāra* of the finite selves, Brahman is the Self that is embodied *(śarīrin)* of the *cit*, the dependent body. This however does not alter the embodied status of *cit;* the relation is only applied at a different and a transcendental level. The finite self in its own right continues to be the embodied self *(śarīrin)* and, therefore, the support *(ādhāra)* of its respective body, which could not continue in existence without the support of the self. In transporting the relation to a transcendental plane, what Rāmānuja has in his mind is that, in its turn, the finite self is supported by a more fundamental reality, namely Brahman, the ultimate *śarīrin*. For the finite selves are also themselves bodies, or parts, of the body of the supreme Self. The supreme Self alone is therefore the ultimate ground *(ādhāra)* of all beings, in particular, the finite conscient beings.

One might ask if Rāmānuja has gained anything by transforming the physical category of 'embodiedness' from its metaphysical to the religious plane. Does not Advaita too make the undifferentiated Brahman the ground of whatever phenomenality that is there? I am inclined to believe that, by this transference, Rāmānuja has liberated metaphysics of its cold and dead categories and infused life and blood, feeling and emotions in them. Thus, the word *ādhāra*, like its English translations 'support' or 'ground', is fundamentally impersonal. It reminds me of an expression, 'God is my Rock', that fails to evoke an Indian religious sensitivity. Rāmānuja must have felt the icy coldness of the category, for he gradually comes to rely on more personal terms such as 'the controller' *(niyantā)* and the principal *(śeṣi)*. Both these terms have much more personal connotation for him in the models that he builds up, as if he were setting a corrective to his own *ādhāra-ādheya* model. These, I shall discuss later; I shall now be concerned with bringing out another aspect of the model at discussion.

There is in the model of *ādhāra-ādheya* an aspect that Rāmānuja strongly emphasises. It is the idea of the divine support for His 'creatures'; thus support to the devotee changes itself into a refuge, a place into which the devotee resorts *(āśraya)*. *Āśraya* thus not merely personalizes the impersonal and the metaphysical *ādhāra* but also highlights the easy availability of God *(saulabhya)* to man. It is Brahman as *āśraya* rather than *ādhāra* that we meet with in the *Gītābhāṣya,* although in *Śrībhāṣya* it is the latter that we meet with, consistent with the spirit of the two works concerned. There however is no contradiction between the two terms, or between their uses in two different works. It is only a difference of intent rather than of content. *Ādhāra* has the philosopher's intent, whereas *āśraya* has the devotee's intent at work. Rāmānuja has shown here a remarkable sense of relevance. But for this, it is the same man who both philosophizes on the truth that Brahman is the ground of his being, and who religiously experiences his utter dependence on God in a very special way. *Ādhāra-ādheya* model has a general metaphysical meaning, which may be said to be, in a sense, the philosophical undercurrent for the models that Rāmānuja speaks of. Therefore, we may even think that the relation of *ādhāra-ādheya* is the first aspect of ontology, or metaphysics, of Viśiṣṭādvaita; and that within its matrix Brahman is viewed as the real of real, or the true of the true *(satyasya-satyaḥ),* the light of lights *(jyotiṣām-jyotiṣ),* the life of life *(prāṇasya-prāṇam)*, the infinite *(ananta)*, the eternal and the imperishable *(akṣara)* and the super-consciousness *(jñāna),* — all the epithets that the *upaniṣads* give to Brahman for the sake of emphasizing the inner unity of the ultimate reality.

The second model of the self-body relationship is that of the ruler-ruled, or the controller-controlled *(niyantā-niyāmya)*. In virtue of this model of relation, Brahman is the ruler, or controller within, of *cit* that is ruled and controlled by Brahman. This conception of the relation between Brahman and *cit* clearly expresses the personal and the dynamic character of God's relation in respect of the world of the conscient selves. To be sure, this relation of ruler to what is ruled also exists between finite selves and their bodies; but Rāmānuja now views it at a different level, as applied to Brahman as the Self and *cit* as his body. For he thinks that the relation is clearly exemplified when God is the self. The verb, *niyam,* has the primary meaning of 'stopping', or 'holding back', and the derived meanings of 'restraining', 'controlling, and 'governing'. From here he has formed the word, *niyantā* (the one who restrains), and applied it to Brahman, or God. What is more, in ordinary parlance, the term *niyantā* can also be applied to a charioteer who guides the chariot by restraining and controlling his horses. It surely is not a coincidence to Rāmānuja that an incarnation *(avatāra)* of God in Kṛṣṇa sanctifies the role of a charioteer in the *Gītā*. Rāmānuja is profoundly moved by this divine condescension towards a lowly man.

Further, it is not merely a desire to draw from a *smṛti* text that has motivated Rāmānuja to use the term *niyantā* to God; the imagery goes back to some of the *Vedic* hymns that may have given rise to the philosophy of Yoga. In all these meanings, *niyantā* admirably suits Rāmānuja's conception of Brahman as *Īśvara* of religion. As *Īśvara,* Brahman is not merely the overlord of all that exists; he rules and controls them from within as the indwelling spirit *(antaryāmīn)*. Just as the rule, or control, is exercised by the self from within over its body, God as *niyantā* of the finite beings may be called *antaryāmīn*, or the 'controller-within', or the 'inner ruler' of the individual self. This name is, in fact, Rāmānuja's favourite name for God. He believes that it adequately, and in a manner that is intrinsically personal, reveals to man God's nature as the Self that animates, rules and controls from within his own body, that is the conscient selves.

For his proof, he relies on the passage from the *Bṛhadāraṇyaka Upaniṣad,* known as the *Antaryāmī-brāhmaṇa,* already quoted in this chapter. 'He who dwells within the Self' *(antar)* is also the 'controller within' *(antaryāmīn)*. The controller within cannot be the finite self *(jīva, cit)*, but the supreme Self, free from all the limitations to which the finite self is heir to. Such a supreme Self is the Brahman of the *upaniṣads*, the Nārāyaṇa of the religions, for he is, as both transcendent and immanent, *puruṣa* that rules all *cit* and *acit,* all the *Vedas*, all divine beings. He thus abides within them, rules over them and within them. If Rāmānuja now makes this Self the *puruṣottama*, he has in the back of his mind not merely the drama unfolded in the *Gītā* but also the tenth *maṇḍala* of the *Ṛg Veda's puruṣa-sūkta*. Against this backdrop we can see the significance of Rāmānuja's words:

> Because the Lord *(Bhagavān)* abides as the Self in all beings, which are His own *vibhūtis*. He may be called by the names of these beings in co-ordinate predication *(samānādhikaraṇya)*, just as the words denoting particular bodies extend in their significance to the souls dwelling in those bodies.[18]

The one significance that stands out in the use of this model for Rāmānuja, closest to his religio-metaphysical heart, is that Brahman, or God, is the core of all beings, irrespective of the stages and phases through which they pass. Thus the totality of beings in Brahman, both active and inert, can exist only in God; apart from God their inner Self, they are a mere nothing. He compares the finite selves to the rays of the sun; as the attributes of the sun, the rays constitute the body of the sun. Likewise the finite selves constitute the body of Brahman or Bhagavān. The light, or the self-consciousness, of the finite *ātman* belongs to Bhagavān, since it is the *vibhūti* and *aṁśa* of Brahman.[19] In conclusion, the model of *niyantā-niyāmya*, expressing the *apṛthak-siddhattva* of *śarīra-śarīri-bhāva*, defines the Brahman of metaphysics as the Īśvara of the ethical religions; the latter is the righteous ruler of the universe, without any taint or caprice, cruelty or evil; and he is the universal redeemer *(sarva-rakṣaka)*.

The third model of the self-body relationship is the relation of the principal and the accessory *(śeṣi-śeṣa)*. In virtue of this model, Brahman is the principal, the primary, or the fundamental, and *cit* is the accessory, the secondary and the subordinate. It is true however that Rāmānuja does not use this model as frequently as the others, although the *Vedārtha-saṁgraha* begins, in its invocatory verse, with this model of *śeṣi* and *śeṣa*, wherein he even indulges in a pun.[20] Yet, it may be noted that the model has highlighted a distinctive aspect of Rāmānuja's metaphysics. Hence, without an explication of this model, our understanding of the soul-body relationship would perhaps be incomplete. For the notion of subservience *(śeṣatva)*, that is inherent in the *śeṣi-śeṣa* relation, is essential for Rāmānuja for defining the self, even as the notion of primacy, that is inherent in the notion of *śeṣitva,* is essential for defining Brahman, the supreme *śeṣin*. For the character of being *śeṣin* is closely linked with the lordship *(īśītṛtva)* and the supremacy *(paratva)* of Brahman over his modes, especially that of *cit*.

The original meaning of the word *śeṣa* is 'remainder'; it is derived from the root *śiṣ,* meaning literally 'to leave', a meaning still retained in the adjectival and the adverbial form *aśeṣa*, 'without remainder', in mathematics; here it has meant negatively 'entire' or 'entirely'. One of the derived meanings of *śeṣa* is 'what is left over', therefore the 'subordinate part', or 'subsidiary', or 'accessory'. It is in this sense that Karma

Mīmāṁsa used the term to describe any subordinate part of the sacrifice, which was intended to serve the principal purpose; and the principal purpose itself of the sacrifice was called *śeṣi*. Rāmānuja makes use of this sense of Karma Mīmāṁsa, when he defines that *śeṣa* is the constituent, or accessory, because it is subservient to another, which may be said to be *śeṣi*. *Śeṣi* is that which possesses *śeṣa,* in virtue of its being the principal element to the accessory elements. It now follows that *śeṣa* is what exists for another, and *śeṣi* is that for which *śeṣa* exists. Sanskrit grammarians too define the terms in a similar way: *śeṣa* is an object possessed, whereas the possessor is *śeṣi*. Rāmānuja seems to be aware of the historical development of these terms, when he places before us the model of *śeṣi-śeṣa-bhāva*.[21]

In the *Vedārtha-saṁgraha*, Rāmānuja, making use of the history of the terms, elaborated on both the principal *(śeṣi)* and the accessory, or the subordinate *(śeṣa)*. He explicates that the *śeṣi-śeṣa* relationship in any situation would imply that *śeṣa* is that whose essential nature consists in being solely useful to something else, by virtue of its intention to contribute some excellence to this other thing; and this other *(paraḥ)* is *śeṣi*. He now proceeds to apply this definition.

The essential nature of all entities, be they eternal or non-eternal, intelligent or non-intelligent, is such that they are solely for the supreme lord. Their value consists in their intention to contribute some excellence to the supreme Brahman, their principal, the governor and the ground. Thus everything is in the state of being subservient *(śeṣa-bhūtam)* to the Lord; and the Lord is the master and owner *(śeṣi)* of everything.[22] Rāmānuja therefore speaks of this model along with the other models of *ādhāra-ādheya* and *niyantā-niyāmya* models, although instances of treating this model itself as expressive of the fundamental soul-body relationship are not altogether absent. But by and large the model seems to be more supplementary than substantial, insofar as it may be said to play a second fiddle to the rest of the models. Thus, for example, in the following verse, *śeṣi-śeṣa-bhāva* is seen supplementary to his understanding of the *śarīraka-śāstra* in terms of the cause and effect, the source and the product:

> These two natures are certainly mine. As everything originates from them, even so they originate from me and belong to me. I alone am their origin; I alone am their dissolution, and I alone am their goal... because I am the cause of the two natures which are the causes of all things, and because I am the *śeṣi*, even of the intelligent beings who are the *śeṣas* of the non-intelligent entities (material defects), I am superior *(paratama)*.[23]

But nothing could be far from the truth, if this supplementary character of *śeṣi-śeṣa* model is construed to be redundant in Rāmānuja's metaphysics. This model, if it seems rather remote to us, it is partly because it is called from the rather archaic practices of ritual Mīmāṁsa, and also partly because the modern consciousness, accustomed to speak of the individual person as an autonomous centre of consciousness and freedom, recoils at the idea of being treated as a disposable property. The model, however, has a distinct purport. Rāmānuja believes that the model of *śeṣi-śeṣa* satisfies the highest demands of ethics and aesthetics, even as the model of *ādhāra-ādheya* satisfies the metaphysical demands, and the model of *niyantṛṇ-niyāmya* satisfies the religious demands. For the model by defining God as the supreme lord *(śeṣi)*, for whose satisfaction the world of *cit* lives, moves, and has its being, has a full bearing on the activity *(pravṛtti)* of *cit*. Indeed, the *cit,* insofar as it is defined to be incapable of any activity *(pravṛtti-anarha)*, is also dependent on supreme Brahman for all its moral conation and the aesthetical creation. Whatever ethical and aesthetical perfection, that the finite self exhibits, is both dependent on the supreme Self, and also redounds to the external glory of the same supreme Self which is the treasure-house of all moral and aesthetical perfections *(sakala-kalyāṇa-aiśvarya-guṇa-nidhaye)*. Therefore the model in question stresses the self-related and the self-realized nature of Brahman, as contrasted with the nature of the finite self that is eternally dependent on Brahman's will. The finite will both exists and works for the satisfaction of the supreme will. Some of the problems that arise from this subordination of human will to the divine will, will be discussed by me later.

Thus we may say that the relation of Brahman and *ātman* as *śarīrin* (soul) and *śarīra* (body) can be explicated by many models; three of them are important. These three models harmonize the three relations, namely, the metaphysical relation of the ground *(ādhāra)* and the consequent *(ādheya)*, the religious relation of the ruler lord *(niyantā)* and the devotee *(niyāmya)*, and the ethico-aesthetical relation of end *(śeṣi)* and means *(śeṣa)*, — all the terms which are only logically distinguishable but not separable. This apparently threefold, but essentially unitary, relation between Brahman and *cit* constitutes the core of Rāmānuja's metaphysics viewed through the perspective of *apṛthak-siddhattva*. Therefore *cit* or *ātman*, is said to be a mode *(prakāra)* of Brahman, *paramātman;* it is thus at once logical, religious, ethical and aesthetical ego to be grasped as the body *(śarīra)* of Brahman, who himself is grasped as the possessor of this cosmic body *(śarīrin)*.

So far my attempt has been to understand Rāmānuja's *śārīraka-śāstra* by analysing it through its models. Equipped with this analytical understanding, we now need to have a synthetic view of the metaphysics of *śārīraka-śāstra,* to which I now turn.

Śarīrin is the possessor of the body *(śarīra),* and is synonymous with *ātman*. It is now applicable to any finite conscient self *(cit)*. But the finite self, to be *śarīrin,* has to fulfil three conditions: The finite self must possess certain modes; the modes must be entirely dependent on the self; and finally they act for the service of the self. Thus *śarīri* is characterized by the body that is determined by modality, dependence and serviceability. When this status of *śarīrin* is extended to Brahman, or when the relation of *śarīri-śarīra* is extended to Brahman and *cit*, there should be the realization of the above three characteristics in this 'elevated' relation, too. What then would happen, if we make the conscient, but the finite, self the body *(śarīra)* of Brahman? Firstly, as a mode it derives its being from Brahman, as the very life of its life *(svarūpāśrita)*; it is sustained by Brahman's immanence *(atmaikaprakāratva)*. Secondly, it is controlled by Brahman's will *(saṁkalpāśrita)*; therefore it absolutely depends on Brahman *(atmaikāśrayatva)*. Finally, it subsists as a means to the realization of the divine purpose *(atmaikaprayojanatra)*; its activity is for the services of Brahman. In this way, being the body of Brahman would mean to *cit* that it derives its substantiality from the Brahman as *ādhāra,* that it depends on his redemptive will as the *niyantṛ* and, above all, that it acts as a means to the service and satisfaction of Brahman. Conversely, what would happen, if we make the supreme Brahman, fully conscient and infinite spirit, the Self *(śarīri)* of the body that is the *cit* ? Firstly, as the substance, it would be the ground of existence for all its modes. Secondly, as the sustainer of its body, it would be entirely independent; and also control the body from within. Finally, it would be the end and goal of its body, insofar as it is the ever fulfilled and realized will, serving as an impetus for all ethical and aesthetical aspirations of its body. In short, Brahman as the *śarīrin* is the source, the sustenance and the satisfaction of the finite self. *Cit*, on the other hand, as *śarīra* is the consequent from Brahman, dependent on Brahman's redemptive will, and agent for the sole satisfaction of Brahman. In this synthetic relation of *śarīri-śarīra, śarīra* 'refers' also to *śarīrin* and vice-versa. Therefore *cit* as *śarīra* of Brahman refers to Brahman as *śarīrin*; likewise Brahman as *śarīri* of *cit* 'refers' to *cit* as *śarīra*.

We should not however overlook the kind of reference that is involved. Though *cit* is different from Brahman in the denotative aspect, as it is a unique individual, it is one with him; hence *cit* connotes Brahman. Again, though Brahman is different from *cit*, he is the substance of *cit;* hence it again connotes *cit* as his mode. Here is the paradox of the relation of *apṛthak-siddhattva*, which seems to reconcile theism with a non-dualism advocated by a Vedāntin. I am afraid, not many scholars have taken note of this important aspect of Rāmānuja's metaphysics.

I have had occasion to state that, in virtue of the threefold models of *śarīri-śarīra-bhāva*, the finite self comes to acquire the status of the logical, the ethical and the aesthetical ego. These are not three egos; rather they are all ultimately transfigured into the threefold expression of *śarīra* of Brahman in terms of *ādheyatva*, *vidheyatva* and *śeṣatva*. For as the logical ego, *cit* derives its substantiality from Brahman, and is called the *apṛthak-siddha viśeṣaṇa, ādheya* and *aṁśa*. As the ethical ego, *cit* is sustained and moved from within, and is called the *apṛthak-siddha niyāmya*. As the aesthetical ego, it dedicates itself to the serive of the lord, and is called *apṛthak-siddha śeṣa,* or *kiṁkara*. Let me bring out the fuller implications of the above statements.

The logical relation of *apṛthak-siddhattva* between the infinite Brahman and the finite self, explicated in terms of *ādhāra-ādheya*, can also be seen as a relation obtained between cause and effect *(kāraṇa-kārya)*, substance and attribute *(guṇī-guṇa)* and also as the whole and the part *(aṁśi-aṁśa)*. Rāmānuja does indeed make use of these categories, although not in the way I have tried to classify them here. *Cit* is the effect *(kārya)* of Brahman, in the sense that a term connoting Brahman is the effected; or differentiated, state *(kārya-brahman)* is coordinated with another term connoting the same

Brahman in the causal, or non-differentiated, state *(kāraṇa-brahman)*. The *satkārya-vādin* that he is, Rāmānuja now views the finite selves as inseparable effects of Brahman, their cause. Brahman now is the ultimate substance *(sat)* which is the locus *(āśraya)* of attributes, that are the finite selves. The finite selves are the attributes *(guṇa)*, that are possessed by their substance *(guṇī)*. Further these selves as *guṇa, viśeṣaṇa*, not only make for the eternal differentiation of the absolute *(sat)*, they also make of themselves eternal parts *(aṁśa)* of Brahman, who is the *vibhu,* the totality. It is here that Rāmānuja thinks of the *upaniṣadic* imagery of *cit* as the eternal sparks of the brilliant self. The one term that he has for it is the mode *(prakāra)* that is at once *ādheya, guṇa* and *aṁśa.* As a mode of Brahman, it is a spiritual 'monad'; the spiritual monad of Rāmānuja must not be interpreted in the quantitative sense. Brahman is *vibhu,* or *virāt;* and he resides immanently in the *monadic cit (aṇu)* as its inner self; and at the same time he exceeds the finite content of the monadic *cit.* Rāmānuja in this way has been successful to reconcile the pluralism of the self with the non-dualism of Brahman, by way of employing the categories of causality, substantiality and infinity that subsume within themselves the categories of effect, attributes and parts respectively. For they all are ultimately traced back to the differentiated Brahman.

The ethical relation of *apṛthak-siddhattva* between Brahman and *cit*, explicated in terms of *niyantā-niyāmya*, stresses the need for reconciliation between the divine transcendence and immanence. Brahman, the supreme *puruṣa,* while transcending all that has risen out of his dismemberment, resides within them and rules them from within. He is the spirit that indwells *(antaryāmīn)*. The individual self is not a mere *viśeṣaṇa*, but an active personality, which is essentially free. But it is a freedom made possible by the immanence of Brahman within the active person of *cit.* Hence, Brahman is the controller *(niyantā)*, the highest spirit *(puruṣottama)*, who makes possible the ethical and religious pursuits of the finite self.

Finally, the aesthetical relation of *apṛthak-siddhattva* between Brahman and *cit*, explicated in terms of *śeṣi-śeṣa,* highlights the truth that the finite self attains self-sovereignty by subjugating its sensibility and egoism *(ahaṁkāra)*, and by dedicating its freedom to the service of Brahman, or Īśvara. The self is to realize its utter dependence *(śeṣatva)* on Īśvara, its inner ruler, and itself as a means *(śeṣa)* to the service and satisfaction of Brahman, who is its *śeṣi*. Rāmānuja firmly believes that *cit* can launch upon the divine end of soul-making only as subservient to its *śeṣi;* hence it has to be fully aware of its status as the servant *(dāsa, kiṁkara)* of the supreme Brahman. The aesthetic relation of *śeṣi-śeṣa* thus reconciles immanence and transcendence of Brahman, by way of making the *cit* realize that it is not only knower *(jñātṛ)*, and the doer *(kartṛ),* but also as the enjoyer *(bhoktṛ)*.

Thus, in conclusion it may be said that the logical view of *apṛthak-siddhattva* promotes between Brahman and *cit* intimacy and unity, the ethical view fosters reverence to, and freedom in, Brahman; and finally the aesthetical view of the same relation combines the two by intuiting Brahman as the transcendent beauty itself *(bhūvana-sundara)*. I am afraid, Rāmānuja's aesthetics is a totally untilled terrain, which however falls outside the purview of this study.

A problem that stands out in the context of the application of the relation of *apṛthak-siddhattva* especially in its model of *niyantā-niyāmya* is that of human freedom vis-a-vis the absolute sovereignty of God. I shall now turn my attention to this problem.

The ethical problem in Rāmānuja's philosophy is the dilemma of determinism: *cit* is either determined by *prakṛti* and its *guṇas*, or controlled by the will of God. In the former case, *cit* is subjected to the powers of materiality and, in the latter case, it is 'swallowed up' by the spirit. Rāmānuja is thus caught between the horns of fatalism and divine overlordship. In either case, the freedom and autonomy of the individual self is at stake. Rāmānuja overcomes the problem by escaping between the horns of the dilemma: he points to the third alternative, namely the freedom of the self on the moral level: The self has the will to attain self-sovereignty to overcome the power of materiality and also to attune its will to that of the supreme divine will.

Rāmānuja has no problem in overcoming fatalism that may be said to be brought about by the subjugation of the self to the materiality. If materiality is understood as *prakṛti,* or *acit*, Rāmānuja does not view it either with suspicion or hostility. It is a *prakāra* of Brahman. It is the marvellous unity of *prakṛti* with Brahman and itself, rather than isolation from Brahman, which characterizes his understanding of the nature of *prakṛti*. While *prakṛti* is the manifested and the external glory of Brahman, it is also what aids the finite self in the process of liberation. This at once indicates that bondage is not, to Rāmānuja, the union with materiality. It is rather the forgetfullness on the part of the self that it is a mode of Brahman. Secondly, if however, *prakṛti* is understood as the concretization of *karma*, Rāmānuja never assigns an independent power to the operation of *karma;* it rather operates as subjected to the will of Brahman.

But the other alternative charge of human freedom being 'swallowed up' by the divine overlordship is philosophically valid. Rāmānuja has to squarely face the problem. Rāmānuja does acknowledge the paradox of human freedom vis-a-vis the divine control. His solution here is that, from the ethico-religious standpoint, human being is free to surrender itself to the will of the supreme Brahman. This at once suggests that he makes a distinction between the freedom at the ontological and freedom at the ethico-religious level. The first may be said to be ontological freedom, the second, moral freedom. In virtue of *cit* being the eternal mode *(prakāra)* of Brahman, there exists the *apṛthak-siddha* relation between Brahman as *niyantā* and *cit* as *niyāmya*. In virtue of this *niyantā-niyāmya* relation, Brahman is the indwelling spirit *(antaryāmīn)*. This relation then bears upon the very nature of *cit*. If so, Rāmānuja concludes that *cit* cannot be said to have any ontological freedom. The ontological separation of Brahman and *cit* is a metaphysical impossibility. But *cit* is morally and religiously free.

Cit then is free only to the ethical and religious extent but, in the ontological sphere however, it is determined. How are we to reconcile this ontological determinism with the ethico religious, or moral freedom? For ontological determinism implies divine premotion in ethico-religious sphere. However unpleasant the situation be, Rāmānuja will not give up the *niyantā* nature of Brahman. He argues that *cit,* insofar as it is *niyāmya*, to be sure, is moved from within; it is a movement that may be said to have come from the inner nature of *cit* itself; therefore it must not be construed as the cancellation of *cit's* moral freedom. Nonetheless, the finite self can say No to the supreme self. This denial is at once a denial of its own nature. Therefore the individual will can come into conflict with the divine will. To the extent it is a negation of its own nature, it is also to that extent a denial of its free nature. Therefore, to Rāmānuja, freedom is fulfilled only in the surrender to the will of the *niyantā Brahman;* it is realized in attuning the finite will to the infinite will, and making itself God's instrument. Thus the *niyāmya* is to transform itself into the perfect *śeṣa*: ethics ultimately is metamorphised into religion.

This transformation of metaphysics into ethics, and of ethics into religion, is because of the inseparable relation between Brahman and *cit*. This relation holds good in bondage and liberation alike. Let me now turn to this final aspect of the application of *apṛthak-siddhattva* between Brahman and *cit*.

It is possible that one may be, specially if he is narrowly positivistic, deeply disturbed with what happens in Rāmānuja's philosophy: His metaphysics crystallizes into a philosophy of religion. This is perhaps due to the fact that he makes no difference between the absolute of philosophy and the God of religion. In doing this, he hopes to reconcile the claims of logic with the needs of religious feelings. We cannot afford to forget that Rāmānuja is not only a metaphysician but also a mystic. When a mystic like Rāmānuja may say that the heart has a logic of its own, this logic is not opposed to the logic of the intellect, because he has already prepared a philosophical ground for its explication. His philosophy therefore not only interprets metaphysics in terms of religion, and religion in terms of metaphysics, but also equates the two by the common designation *darśana*.

This composite meaning of *darśana* at once includes within itself sacrality, reality and value into a single unity. This way he has succeeded in synthesizing the conflicting claims of *upaniṣadic* non-dualism with the *Vedic* and the non-*Vedic* theism. His seems to be a brilliant integration of the many philosophical, scriptural and traditional trends of the Indian culture of his days. Whether we understand Rāmānuja's philosophy as metaphysics or religion and exegesis or culture, he is keen to retain, at everyone of these levels, the distinct status of his *tattva-traya,* namely Brahman, *cit* and *acit*. But this distinction is to be understood within the Vedāntic context.

Hence, the relation between them is one of inseparability. This inseparability refers to the very nature of the realities that he speaks of. The relation that holds between Brahman and *cit*, in particular, is valid at the level of metaphysics, ethics, religion and of aesthetics. Hence, this relation may be said to hold good at all times. Hence the finite self is related inseparably with Brahman not only in bondage *(bandha)*, not only when it is concorporated *(prākṛtika)*, not only when it is set on the path of liberation *(mumukṣu),* but also when it is ultimately freed *(mukta)* and enjoys the company of the ultimate Brahman, the Nārāyaṇa of religion. Liberation is neither the cancellation of the distinct identity of *cit,* by way of a merger with Brahman's essence, nor a realization of *cit* as an unrelated entity. It is rather a rediscovering of one's identity as inseparably rooted in the nature of the ultimate Brahman. In this sense, *apṛthak-siddhattva* is an eternal, intrinsic and organismic relation.[24]

References

1. *Śrībhāṣya,* 1.1.1.
2. *Vedārtha-saṁgraha,* 20.
3. *Ibid.*, 17.
4. *Śvetāśvatara Upaniṣad*, 1.6, 1.9, VI.9, 13, 16; *Bhagavadgītā*, II.12; *Śrībhāṣya*, II.1.22.
5. *Bhagavadgītā,* XV.7.
6. *Śrībhāṣya,* II. 3.42-45.
7. *Chāndogya Upaniṣad*, III.12.6.
8. *Śrībhāṣya,* .1.1.1.
9. *Ibid.*,1.1.12.
10. *Ibid.*, 2.1.9.
11. *Gītābhāṣya*, 10.20.
12. *Ibid.*, 7.12.
13. *Śrībhāṣya*, 2.1.23.
14. *Ibid.*, 1.4.37.
15. *Ibid.*, 1.1.13.
16. *Vedārtha-saṁgraha*, 11; *Chāndogya Upaniṣad*, VI. 1.4.
17. *Gītābhāṣya*, 7.19.
18. *Bhagavadgītā, Vibhūtiyoga,* 10: 21-38.

19. *Gītābhāṣya,* 15.6.
20. *Vedārtha-saṁgraha* 1: *Aśeṣa-cidacidvastu-śeṣiṇeśeṣāyiṇe...*
21. *Vedārtha-saṁgraha*, 121.
22. *Ibid.*, 121-22.
23. *Gītābhāṣya,* 7.6; *Vedārtha-saṁgraha,* 76, 80, 83, 90, 97, 106.
24. It would be of some interest to see if *apṛthak-siddhi* relation is also applicable between Śrī and Nārāyaṇa. Śrī does not seem to have been presented by Rāmānuja as an independent *tattva*, but only as an aspect of Nārāyaṇa. Śrī is depicted as the maternal aspect of the God of religion. Therefore the relation that holds between the two may be said to be of identity rather than inseparability between the distinct eternal entities. Treatment of this issue would be of interest to a philosopher of religion; it however falls outside the purview of my book.

6

Conclusion

In concluding this study instead of merely summing up in earlier chapters, a few reflections on Rāmānuja's method would perhaps put me on the path of deeper studies in the area in the coming years. Such an attempt may also be warranted to some extent, in the context of the efforts to look Rāmānuja's metaphysics from the perspective of a unique relation that goes by the name of *apṛthak-siddhattva*. This enterprise on methodology seems to be further warranted by conviction that Vedānta, in its many forms, in particular, those advocated by Śaṁkara and Rāmānuja, is fundamentally a hermeneutics, or a scriptural exegesis. If so, what is Rāmānuja's approach to a philosophy seen as a hermeneutics?

The three points have been highlighted here. In the first place, Rāmānuja builds upon the Naiyāyikas without being a crass realist. This is made possible by his 'inductive'[1] approach within Vedānta. Secondly, his integrative method has made possible the unity of the opposites in the self as well as the highest reality. Thirdly, he has a marvellous sensitivity to historicity in his hermeneutics; this has made possible the synthesis of metaphysics and religion.

'Vedānta' may be taken in two senses: firstly, it may mean, literally, the concluding part of the *Vedic* lore. Understood in this sense, the *upaniṣads* constitute the concluding portion of the *Veda*; Vedānta here would therefore mean the philosophy of the *upaniṣads*. Secondly, it may mean 'the end' or 'the goal' of the *Vedas*. Understood this way, it may mean a philosophy of human life and liberation, since these items constitute the core of the teaching of the *Veda*. Initially an affirmation and a negation on a phenomenal level and, again, a re-affirmation on a transcendental level, of human existence, characterize the Vedāntic philosophy. What kind of Vedāntic hermeneutics may Rāmānuja be said to be doing?

Śaṁkara is a transcendentalist par excellence. He begins with the non-dual Brahman as his basic postulate, and thence from the 'high heavens' of the *pāramārthika*, he descends to explicate his philosophy of non-dualism *(advaita)*. His approach may be said, in a sense, 'deductive'. His vision is *sub specie aeternitatis*. From his basic postulate of *brahma-satyaṁ,* he derives his philosophy of the world and the individual self. *Mithyātva* of *jagat* and the *na-paratva* of *jīva* are the derivative truths *(dṛṣṭi)*. They constitute the realm of practicality, or empiricality *(vyavahāra)*. As derivative, they are merely secondary, and are a mere concession to our practicality. Human existence, in its aspect of life and liberation, is to be assigned meaning from the perspective of a transcendental truth *(pāramārthika-sattā)*. Naturally, the meanings that are assigned to the world and the self, nay more, even to God, if such a reality is admitted, are relative, for they are still the products of the nescience *(avidyā-māyā)*. I shall call this method a transcendental hermeneutics.

As distinct from Śaṁkara's approach, Rāmānuja may be said to be an immanentalist. While he too may be said to subscribe to the conception of a basic non-dual reality, he does not start his philosophy with this postulate. His postulate is a concrete reality immanented in the world of the conscient *(cit)* and the inconscient *(acit)* entities. He begins his philosophy with the plurality of the finite selves and the world of objects, and ascends to a transcendentalism, that however does not cancel the realities of *cit* and *acit,* at any stage. He rather takes the realities of *cit* and *acit,* in themselves complete and total in terms of their reality, and deposits them in the heart of the reality. This is because, in his view, in the ultimate reality *cit* and *acit* are eternally co-eval, in a relation of inseparability *(apṛthak-siddhattva)* with the ultimate reality.

Hence, Rāmānuja's approach, in a sense, may be said to be 'inductive'. He analyses the world of the conscient and the inconscient as given, and traces them back to their ontic ground, Brahman. In terms of reality *(sat)* itself, there is no question of primary and secondary realities here. They are co-eval. Yet, in virtue of the utter dependence of *cit* and *acit* on Brahman, an ontic priority, not in terms of time or their essence at any rate, is assigned to Brahman, whose modes *(prakāra)* they are said to be. The world of the inconscient *(acit)* is neither illusory nor unreal. Likewise, the world of the conscient selves *(cit)* is not identical in essence with the supreme transcendental reality. They have fullness or completion of essence in themselves, although they are eternally dependent on Brahman. Hence, they are not derivative realities, in the sense that they are entertained as existent only to cater to our practicality and then sublated to affirm the reality of the transcendental reality. Their affirmation does not negate the reality of the ultimate, because they constitute Brahman's body. Likewise, the affirmation of the reality of Brahman too does not call for the minimization of the reality of the finite selves or the material world, much less their cancellation. Therefore Rāmānuja does not indulge in the distinction between the *pāramārthika* and the *vyāvahārika*. Our practicality has as much significance as anything else. Because Rāmānuja begins his philosophy with what is immediately given to our experience, and then moves on to the transcendental reality as the ontic ground *(ādhāra)*, he is much more 'inductive' in his approach to a philosophy of reality. I shall call this an immanental hermeneutics, rather than empirical hermeneutics, as distinct from Śaṁkara's transcendental hermeneutics.

I am inclined to believe that it is in virtue of the immanental hermeneutics that Rāmānuja is capable of avoiding the crass realism of Nyāya. The crass realism of Nyāya made it accept inherence *(samavāya)* as a distinct category. In the Naiyāyika's relation of substance-attribute. *(guṇa-guṇī, kriyā-kriyāvān)*, neither attribute nor action, both of which need a substratum for their being, is endowed with consciousness *(cit)*. There is a radical difference here between *apṛthak-siddhi-bhāva* of Rāmānuja and *samavāya* of Nyāya,— a difference that has facilitated Rāmānuja to avoid the pitfalls of crass realism, and also to remain a Vedāntin, and thus to safeguard a realistic pluralism within the Vedāntic tradition. *Cit* and *acit* are distinct, total in themselves, yet reside in the supreme Self inseparably; in virtue of inseparability, they are the modes and attributes of Brahman.

It is not the case that the Naiyāyikas do not have the concept of separability *(pṛthak-bhāva)*. But this *pṛthak-bhāva* is synonymous with *vibhāga*. It is a relation that is applicable to the physical materiality. In this sense, it may be said to be a physical category. If they speak of *apṛthak-bhāva*, it merely stands for the indivisibility *(avibhāga)* of the ultimate material atoms. But, for Rāmānuja the category of *apṛthak-bhāva* is what is applied to the metaphysical entities of Brahman, *cit* and *acit*. It provides for distinctness as well as inseparability between the entities concerned. Such a relational category holds good among entities that are eternal and organismic. It at once provides for the fulfilment of metaphysics, ethics, religion and aesthetics.

In virtue of this unique relation, the metaphysical entities, that it relates, are in their totality themselves and yet inseparable from one another. It is in a sense a supra-logical equation that the scriptures speak of in such verses as: That one is total; This one is total: from the total, the total is subtracted and, what is left over is the total; add to That one This one, and the sum total is totality. The ultimate Brahman is qualified by the eternal distinctiveness of individual selves and the matter as its attributes. Such a relationship is unique, and cannot be exemplified by anything realized in our world of experience, in spite of Rāmānuja's attempt to explicate it by way of some of the familiar models. We cannot therefore find fault with Rāmānuja when he finally insists on the need for a *sādhana* of *prapatti*, at once ritual, ethical, religious and mystical, not only to figure out but also to participate in that unique relationship with the ultimate Brahman. In passing from logic and metaphysics to religion, through this relation of *apṛthak-siddhattva*, Rāmānuja has not only fulfilled his logical propensities as a philosopher but also left room for mystical union of self with God. The *ādhāra-ādheya-bhāva* thus transforms into *śeṣi-śeṣa-bhāva*, divesting the former of its icy coldness and filling it with the warmth of love therein.

Secondly, Rāmānuja's method has made possible a unity of the opposites in the world of the inconscient *(acit)*, the conscient *(cit)* and, above all, in Brahman.

That the world is a unity of many forces and currents often antagonistic to one another, is directly given to our experience. The world is a unity of diversely opposite forces. The world-process of conflicting forces is traced by Rāmānuja to the three elements of earth, water and fire. Their unity however is traced back to the single principle of *prakṛti*, that manifests first of all into the elements cited, to give rise to the multiplicity of the world of objects by way of triplication *(trivṛtkaraṇa)*. Further, *prakṛti* itself is the great vibrating matter in virtue of its *guṇas* of *sattva, rajas* and *tamas*. And yet, their unity is once again traced back to the fact that *prakṛti*.

or *acit*, is a mode of Brahman; it is grounded in the ultimate reality of Brahman. The unity of Brahman ultimately bespeaks the unity of the world in the midst of its multiplicity.

Even so, Rāmānuja sees the conscient self *(cit)* as a marvellous synthesis of the opposite within itself. This is so, not only in the sense of its being an organic unity of the body and soul, but also in the sense of being a locus of conflicting propensities within the finite self. Thus, he does not see any conflict in *cit* being both the bonded self *(baddha)* and at the same time an entity that intensely longs for liberation *(mumukṣu)*. The self thus is at once the 'sinner' and the 'saint'. It can enjoy moral freedom and, yet, is ontically rooted in Brahman. As an ontological entity the human self experiences all those self-divisions within itself and, yet, authentically experiences its own unity. Within it can thus exist *baddhatva* and *mumukṣatva* side by side. This is made possible because it is a mode of Brahman and therefore a replica of Brahman. Brahman himself admits within himself the unity of differentiated modes, distinct but seemingly possessing mutually exclusive characteristics.

The above synthesis of the seeming contradictions, within the world of the conscient self *(cit)*, the inconscient world *(acit)* and also within the transcendental reality itself, has important bearings on the methodology of Rāmānuja.

It may perhaps be stated with a certain degree of certainty that Rāmānuja was the first intellectual in the history of the Vedāntic hermeneutics to have detected the serious flaws in the exposition of the *upaniṣadic* ontology, especially as presented by *Śaṁkara*. Though it is true that a ground was prepared for such a hermeneutics by many other thinkers, notable among them being Yāmuna, Rāmānuja was the first to put his *bhakti-paraṁpara* on a scriptural footing. He thus gained for *bhakti*, a philosophical and scriptural status, that was however so far treated among the intellectuals with a derision, as if *bhakti* were a mere concession made to the lesser intellects. Rāmānuja not only drew from his local, often non-*Vedic* tradition, but also traced the elements of *bhakti* and theism to the *upaniṣadic* teaching itself. Convinced of the *śabdha-prāmāṇyatva*, he did not feel the need to write commentaries on any of the *upaniṣads* which other *ācāryas* within Vedānta seemed to have done. But, his belief in the authority of the Vedic scripture is beyond any doubt, insofar as he abundantly quotes from them.

A concept with which Rāmānuja is unusually concerned is *kaivalya,* or liberation, understood in the sense of spiritual isolation. Śaṁkara's doctrine of *kaivalya* made no sense to Rāmānuja who could speak of *baddahatva* and *mumukṣutva* within the same *cit,* or who could speak of the unity of Brahman, *cit* and *acit*. If he rejected this notion of *kaivalya* it is not only because he wanted to safeguard the autonomy of the self but also because he believed that autonomy is ultimately significant only within heteronomy. After all, he was a philosopher of relatedness. He would say that relatedness is not only within *acit* and *cit* but also within Brahman, however logically conceived relatedness seemed to harbour the ideas of logical opposites. The need for logical opposites within the self, after the manner of the supreme Self, that is a unity in the midst of diversity, seems to stem from the religious propensity of the self that seeks salvation through *bhakti*. In this context, *kaivalya* seemed to Rāmānuja opposed to *bhakti*, for *kaivalya* bespeaks of isolation, stagnation and spiritual petrification. In *kaivalya*, the individual self would be bereft of all movements of body, mind and self; thus at once *kaivalya* would also be opposed to *karma* and *jñāna* alike. Hence, Rāmānuja spoke against the sway of *kaivalya* in Vedānta and advocated inter-relationship between not only *cit, acit,* and Brahman, but also between *cit* and *cit*, thus providing for an intersubjectivity within the Vedāntic context. It is this second aspect of his inter-relationship that can be fruitfully be explored as a basis for a social philosophy. The inter-relatedness in

Brahman thus becomes a model for the inter-relatedness within the human community, because we are members of one another, all united in the ontic synthesis of Brahman, or within divinity itself. Now, the concept of salvation acquires new nuances; it is not merely spiritual but also social.

Finally, it brings out the marvellous sensitivity of Rāmānuja to historicity, exhibited in his hermeneutics. This has contributed not a little to an integration of the Indian society. This inestimable social value comes to us from Rāmānuja's attempt at incorporating historicity, or culture, in his philosophical methodology.

In the Vedāntic history, Rāmānuja comes on the scene three centuries after Śaṁkara. We have to acknowledge ungrudgingly that Śaṁkara was a doyen of Vedānta, indeed one of the greatest metaphysician that India has ever known. His interpretation of Vedānta in terms of non-dualism, in the eighth century seemed to have said the last word on Vedāntic philosophy. If so, where was the need for Rāmānuja in the eleventh century to come up with a novel interpretation of Vedānta, and that too, in direct opposition to Śaṁkara? Would he size up to the towering intellectual genius of Śaṁkara, if he directly opposed the doctrine of non-dualism?

The need for a reinterpretation of Vedānta was felt deeply at the grass-root level of the Indian society. Śaṁkara's metaphysics soon came to be viewed as deficient religiously. It was seen to be not catering to the spirituality of the common man. Śaṁkara was thought of as having created an ivory tower of scholasticism for the select few *jñānis*. The common man's spirituality felt increasingly alienated from the Vedāntic metaphysics. They felt that Śaṁkara's metaphysical edifice did not make any room for them. Whatever the grievance be here, it cannot be said that common man needed no guidance in matters of life and liberation. What is more, for them life and liberation ought to be homogeneously juxtaposed; they cannot at any stage be sundered by an artificial division between the realm of truth and the realm of practicalities. Rāmānuja was the philosopher of the time to reinterpret Vedānta for the common man.

This he did superbly with a profound sensitivity to time and place in which he was placed. Therefore in a sense, his philosophy is also a philosophy of culture. By intellectual training, he belonged to a Sanskritic tradition, but by birth he was placed in a milieu that was substantially non-Sanskritic. He was well-read in the Sanskritic philosophy of the time, especially Advaita; but by religious practice, he was a sectarian Vaiṣṇava. Thus he was the man with his head soaring high in the Vedāntic tradition, but feet firmly planted in his local soil. He was the philosopher of the spirit but, at the same time, a man of the world and God. This made it possible for him to combine his brand of Vedānta with the mysticism of the Tamil poet saints *Āḷvārs*. Thus, he did not discard any of the religio-metaphysical resources that were available to him in the society. He discarded nothing as irrelevant to the 'ultimate concern' of man. Therefore, we see in him both a metaphysician and a religionist; it is difficult to separate these two aspects from his life and philosophy.

With this comprehensive attitude to the ultimate concern, he paid close attention to the non-Sanskritic history of his native soil. He imbibed from the *Āḷvārs* the spirit of the *Drāviḍa-veda*, and incorporated it in his Vedānta. Religion thus became to him in a true Indian sense *Dharma*. It is all that holds and maintains humanity at large in a place *(dhāraṇād-dharma ity-ahuḥ)*. Thus what his birth had given him by way of his milieu was meaningfully incorporated and integrated into the intellectual tradition of the *Veda*. Not only this, he enlarged the scope of *smṛti* and drew his inspiration freely, not only from the *Bhagavad-gītā*, but also from the *Pāñcarātra* and the *Bhāgavata-purāṇa*. He may be said to be a pioneer in the process of integration of the Drāviḍian spirituality with the philosophy of Vedānta.

This marked a glorious beginning of a new Vedāntic hermeneutics. A Hindu syncretism may be said to emerge with such fusion of the elements of the *Vedic-Brahmanic-Upaniṣadic* philosophy with all those indigeneous religio-cultural heritage, from the installing of the *Vedic* deities on the totemic animals to iconic worship and rituals in the temples. At a time when the caste structure was sacrosanct in a society, Rāmānuja opposed it in no unmistakable terms, on the ground that an integral liberation is the birth-right of everyman, high-born as much as the low-born. He asserted the equality of men, because as the conscient mode of Brahman, they constituted a spiritual community that is at once God's body. Further, in Śaṁkara's philosophy God had no ultimate significance, though not missing entirely. For God too, to Śaṁkara, is a product of nescience; world is a dream-play; and, above all, the emotive side of man was relegated to the manifestation of either passion or inertia *(rājasika, tāmasika)*.

Such a philosophy for the common man is anything but elevating; it is, if anything, depressive; for the common man, who sets on the path of liberation, is in the midst of the world; the world is concorporated with and around him. Rāmānuja wisely filled up the missing gaps of Śaṁkara's Vedānta, and restructured the Vedāntic thought. He is a Vedāntin, not merely in the traditional sense, but also in the sense of one who has integrated his indigeneous spirituality with that of the *Veda*. He is thus rightly hailed to be the *ubhaya-vedāntin*. His attempts at synthesizing the personal God of the indigeneous spirituality, (a personal God is not entirely absent in the *upaniṣads* though), with the impersonal Brahman of the *upaniṣads* was happily welcomed by the intellectuals of the Sanskritic tradition and the common man alike. In particular, his attempts at establishing the *bhakti-yoga* as a *sādhana* par excellence, and at transforming it into *prapatti*, as a way of total surrender to God, spoke directly to the religious aspirations of the common man. Rāmānuja could achieve all these goals by being a *ubhaya-vedāntin*. If we have anything to learn fruitfully from this method of Rāmānuja is this integrative approach in a society that every now and then exhibits the upsurges of the disintegrative tendencies in a pluralistic society on the basis of caste, creed and religious ideologies.

Even within the Sanskritic tradition itself, he showed this integrative approach by going beyond the notion of a narrow and strict scripturality. In his philosophical system he extended the meaning of Vedānta by drawing inspiration from the post-*upaniṣadic smṛti* literature of the *purāṇas,* the *āgamas* and the mystical poetry. This way he made Vedānta flexible in order that it could respond to the needs of the society. As a hermeneutician, he succeeded in stretching the notion of scriptures beyond the *upaniṣadic* texts. He did not view the post-*upaniṣadic* literature as merely 'secular' writings; he saw in them the authority of the living word embodying the spirit of the scriptures, as they manifest in the lives of men in the world. Hence his understanding of the scripture is dynamic; he refused to see the scriptures as a petrified writ.

What is more, even within the notion of the strict scripturality, he exhibited the above synthetic and integrative approach. Having made the metaphysical highest identical with the religious highest, he provided for a God who would be accessible to man at the 'level of essence'. This God is the *Puruṣ ottama,* the *Saguṇa Brahman,* without being a lower level reality as it was with Advaita, but who accepts man's *sādhanas* of *karma, jñāna* and *bhakti*. While Rāmānuja integrated *karma* and *jñāna* with *bhakti*, as a single *sādhana* of *karma-jñāna-bhakti-samuccaya,* his unique approach to *karma* deserves a close look.

His approach made for the resolution of the conflict between the two Mīmāṁsa viz. *Karma Mīmāṁsa* and *Jñāna*

Mīmāṁsa, or Vedānta. By advocating *karma-sannyāsa,* in preference for knowledge, as the sole means of liberation *(jñāna eva)*, Advaitin had driven a wedge into the authority of the scriptures. *Śāstra,* to him, had come to mean not the earlier part of the scriptures which dealt with the *karma-kāṇḍa*, but only the latter part, which dealt with the *jñāna-kāṇḍa.* This way the Advaitic approach had selectively given the status of scripture, even within the orthodox understanding of scripturality, only to the *jñāna-kāṇḍa*. Rāmānuja, on the other hand, viewed the scriptural authority as single *(eka-śāstra).* His vision was to have far reaching impact for Hindu philosophy and religion. Following the *Gītā*, he may be said to have transformed the *karma-kāṇḍa* into a devoted and disinterested service to God; it is now a service without hankering for the fruits of action. Thus, the *karma-kāṇḍa* is not confined to its narrow ritualism, it is 'sublimated' as service done in tender love for one's God and his people. Thus the *karma-sannyāsa* of Advaitin is raised to a higher level, and given the status of *niṣkāma-karma* of the *Gītā*. Even this disinterested service is divested of its negative connotation by transforming it into a *prapatti-kaiṅkarya*. The net result of all this is that he is now in a position to acknowledge the integrality of the scriptures without driving a wedge into it. This too is a significant contribution that is made possible by his synthetic approach in hermeneutical enterprise.

References

1. Author does not want anyone to identify the terms 'inductive' and 'deductive' with their corresponding methods in the western logic.. The reference here is only two *approaches* to reality rather than scientific methods.

Bibliography

Primary Sources

Ayyangar Narasimha, M.B., *Vedāntasāra of Bhagavad Rāmānuja*, Madras: The Adyar Library, 1953.

Bhattanathaswamy, *Vedāntadeepa: A Gloss on Brahmasūtra,* by Śrī Bhagavat Rāmānujāchārya, Benaras: Messers Braj B. Das and Co., 1904.

Buitenen, J.A.B. Van, *Rāmānuja on the Bhagavat Gītā*, Delhi: Motilal Banarsidass, 1974.

—, *Vedārthasaṁgraha*, Poona: Deccan College Postgraduate and Research Institute, 1956.

Karmarkar, R.D., *Śrībhāṣya of Rāmānuja,* Vol. I, 3 parts, Poona: University of Poona, 1959, 1962, 1964.

Müller, F. Max., Edt., *Sacred Books of the East*, Series Vol. XLVIII, Trans. by G. Thibaut, Oxford University Press, 1904, Delhi: Motilal Banarsidass, reprinted 1962.

Raghavachar, S.S., *Vedārthasaṁgraha*, Text and Translation, Mysore: Ramakrishna Ashram, 1956.

Sudarshanacharya, T.K.V.N., *Vedārthasaṁgraha of Rāmānujachārya with the Commentary Tātparyadīpikā of Śrī Sudarśana-bhaṭṭa*, Oriental Institute, 1953.

Sampatkumaran, M.R., *The Gītābhāṣya of Rāmānuja,* Madras: Rangacharya Memorial Trust, 1969.

Swamy Annangaracharya, *Śrī Bhagavad Rāmānuja Granthamālā,* Kancheepuram: Granthamālā Office, 1956.

Sastri P.S. Rammisra, *Vedārthasaṁgraha with the Gloss Tātparya-dīpikā*, Benaras: Lazarus and Co., 1924.

Secondary Sources

Apte, V.M., *Brahma-Sūtra: Śaṁkara Bhāṣya,* Bombay: Popular Books Depot, 1960.

Bhattacharjee, A., *Studies in Post-Śaṁkara Dialectics*, Calcutta: University of Calcutta, 1936.

Bhatt, S.R., *Studies in Rāmānuja Vedānta,* New Delhi: Heritage Publishers, 1975.

Carman, J.B., *The Theology of Rāmāṇuja,* The New Haven and London: Yale University Press, 1974.

Chatterjee, S. and Datta, D., *An Introduction to Indian Philosophy,* Calcutta: University of Calcutta, 1984.

Chakravarty, V.R. Srisaila., *The Philosophy of Śrī Rāmānuja,* Madras: V.S.R. Chakravarty, 1974.

Chari, S.M. Srinivasa., *Advaita and Viśiṣṭādvaita,* New Delhi: Asia Publishing House, 1961.

Dasgupta, S.N., *A History of Indian Philosophy,* Vol. III, Cambridge, 1952.

Date, V.H., *Vedānta Explained: Śaṁkara's Commentary on the Brahma Sūtras,* Vol. II. Benaras: Munshiram Manoharlal Publishers Pvt. Ltd., 1954.

Deussen, P., *The Philosophy of the Upaniṣads,* New York: Dover Publications Inc, 1966.

Ghate, V.S., *The Vedānta: A Study of the Brahmasūtras with the Bhāṣya of Śaṁkara, Rāmānuja, Nimbārka, Madhva and Vallabha,* Poona: The Bhandarkar Oriental Series, 1960.

Gupta Anima Sen, *A Critical Study of the Philosophy of Rāmānuja,* Varanasi: The Chowkhamba Sanskrit Series, 1967.

Hiriyanna, M., *Outlines of Indian Philosophy*, London: George Allen and Unwin, 1958.

Jariwalla, Y.S., *Gītā: The Science of Living,* Delhi: Motilal Banarsidass, 1984.

Kumarappa, B., *The Hindu Conception of Deity as Culminating in Rāmānuja,* London: Luzac & Co., 1934.

Lott, J. Eric., *God and the Universe in the Vedānta Theology of Rāmānuja,* Madras: Rāmānuja Research Society, 1976.

Radhakrishnan, S., *Brahma Sūtra,* Trans. with an introduction and notes, London: George Allen and Unwin Ltd., 1960.

—, *The Vedānta According to Śaṁkara and Rāmānuja*, London: George Allen and Unwin Ltd., 1928.

Raghavachar, S.S., *Śrī Rāmānuja on the Upaniṣads,* Madras: Prof. M. Rangacharya Memorial Trust, 1972.

Shastri, M.N., *Hindu Metaphysics,* New Delhi: Cosmo Publications, 1978.

Sharma, C.D., *A Critical Survey of Indian Philosophy,* Delhi: Motilal Banarsidass, 1976.

Singh, B., *Foundations of Indian Philosophy,* New Delhi: Orient Longman Ltd., 1971.

Srinivasachari, P.N., *The Philosophy of Viśiṣṭādvaita*, Madras: The Adyar Library and Research Centre, 1978.

Srivastava S.N.L., *Śaṁkara and Bradley,* Delhi: Motilal Banarsidass, 1968.

Stecherbatsky, T., *Buddhist Logic,* Vol. I, New York: Dover Publications, Inc., 1962.

Twenty-four Erudite Scholars, *Viśiṣṭādvaita Philosophy and Religion: A Symposium,* Madras: Rāmānuja Research Society, 1974.

Varadachari, K.C., *Viśiṣṭādvaita and its Development,* Tirupati: Chakravarty Publications, 1969.

Index